THE GOOD NEIGHBOR COOK BOOK

THE GOOD NEIGHBOR COOKBOOK

125 Easy and Delicious Recipes to Surprise and Satisfy the New Moms, New Neighbors, Recuperating Friends, Community-Meeting Members, Book Club Cohorts, and Block Party Pals in Your Life!

Sara Quessenberry

and

Suzanne Schlosberg

Andrews McMeel
Publishing, LLC

Kansas City · Sydney · London

**To all of the good neighbors who have gone
the extra mile for us in the kitchen**

Contents

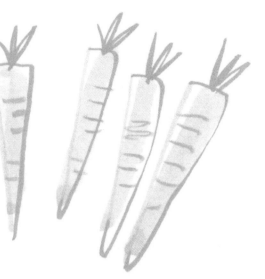

Introduction   viii

Chapter 1   Bringing Home Baby   1

Chapter 2   Get Well Soon   35

Chapter 3   Welcome to the Neighborhood   59

Chapter 4   Block Parties and Barbecues   83

Chapter 5   Meet and Eat: Community, Religious,
and Business Gatherings   111

Chapter 6   Novel Ideas for Book Clubs   131

Chapter 7   Condolences   153

Acknowledgments   175

Metric Conversions and Equivalents   178

Index   182

Introduction

by Suzanne Schlosberg

A week after my husband and I brought our twin boys home from the hospital, a pot of gorgeous three-bean chili appeared, mysteriously, on our doorstep. We felt—and I'm barely exaggerating—as if we had won the lottery. Overwhelmed and wiped out, we'd been eating cereal for dinner and snacking on peanut butter spooned from the jar. We devoured that chili within the hour, even before learning who'd dropped it off, and I decided then that when my life got less topsy-turvy, I'd help out other new moms the same way.

A few months later, I began signing up, through a local club, to bring meals to families of newborn twins and triplets. But I am no chef, and I was perpetually short on ideas, not to mention time. Once, I was so rushed that I brought cold, store-bought quiche. Another time I drew a blank and sheepishly delivered a take-out pizza.

Eventually, I got the chili recipe from the friend who'd rescued us, and that chili became my go-to dish for parents of newborns. But one recipe doesn't fit all occasions, and there are so many occasions that inspire us to contribute a dish or deliver a meal.

We've all faced the good-neighbor dilemma: We want to say "I care" or "I'm thinking of you" or "Hey, I'm no slacker!" by showing up with delicious homemade food. But with hectic schedules, we often have enough trouble getting our own dinners to the table. Who has time to pull together a meal for the new family down the street or a memorable appetizer for the book club potluck? Most of us have been to meetings where the heartiest breakfast fare is an assortment of doughnut holes or attended block parties where the food spread consists of a bowl of potato chips with dairy-case onion dip and a bag of corn chips with bottled salsa.

I'm well acquainted with this culinary crisis. Fortunately, my partner in creating this cookbook, Sara Quessenberry, is eminently qualified to solve it. An accomplished chef with an eye for fresh ingredients and inventive flavor combinations, Sara rescues time-strapped cooks day in and day out at *Real Simple*.

Together we've fashioned a book that offers one-stop recipe shopping for any good neighbor. Sara's recipes, all easy to transport, are uniquely designed to nourish old and new friends—the exhausted mom nursing a newborn, the friend who's feeling under the weather, the couple who just moved in down the block, the family in mourning. The recipes here will make a hero out of anyone attending a PTA meeting, Fourth of July barbecue, church potluck, or business breakfast.

How This Book Is Organized

Our chapters are organized by occasion rather than by food category, on the theory that when you're heading to a block party, you don't think, "What chicken dish should I bring?" Instead, you wonder, "What the heck can I whip up in the least amount of time that suits the event?" The book's handy structure helps you make that decision quickly and easily.

Within each chapter, you'll find a wide variety of dishes perfectly matched to the occasion. We have included high-energy snacks for nursing moms, nutrient-packed soups for recuperating friends, elegant appetizers for book club meetings, and substantial breakfast fare for morning get-togethers. Of course, you can mix and match from various chapters. The Zucchini and Parmesan Frittata, from chapter 2, Get Well Soon, will delight any new mom hankering for a snack. Likewise, the Raspberry-Rhubarb Crumble Pie from chapter 3, Welcome to the Neighborhood, will be a knockout at any block party or barbecue.

Though there's nothing too wild or fancy here, the recipes offer a fresh take on many classics and party favorites. Instead of showing up to that Labor Day barbecue with a bowl of ordinary spinach dip, you'll wow the crowd with your Chipotle-Pineapple Guacamole (page 86). And while new neighbors would be thrilled to receive any plate of cookies, the new folks on your street will be doubly delighted by the gift of Lemon-Glazed Pistachio Shortbread Cookies (page 76).

Homemade food is a labor of love, but it need not be laborious. Sara's recipes are straightforward and easy to follow, and when you've finished making Creamy Tomato Baked Ravioli and Spinach (page 21) or Brown Butter Blueberry Muffins (page 33), your kitchen won't look like it's been ransacked by a bunch of toddlers. You won't find an ingredients list that's unpronounceable or a mile long; what you will find, on occasion, are some wonderful ingredients, such as Swiss chard, parsnips, and quinoa, which you may not cook with regularly.

You also will find tips for making dishes in advance, storing them in the refrigerator or freezer, and transporting them—spill-free—to a get-together. For occasions when you're in a rush, we offer time-saving options such as using a rotisserie chicken rather than roasting your own or using or substituting store-bought enchilada sauce or pasta sauce for Sara's homemade versions. When you simply don't have time to heat up the oven, we've included ideas for even shorter shortcuts, such as assembling a beautiful cheese platter (see page 139) and creating a lovely appetizer spread from ingredients that you can pick up at the supermarket (see page 125). Conversely, when you're able to go the extra mile, flip to our tips on organizing a meal train, whether for a new mom or a grieving family (see page 19), and in chapter 2, Six More Ways to Nourish a Friend on the Mend (page 44).

I still bring three-bean chili to parents of newborn twins every so often, but thanks to Sara I now have a large repertoire of hassle-free dishes that I can count on to be a comfort and a treat. This includes my latest go-to meal, Sara's Sweet Pepper and Spinach Lasagne (page 166); it's especially delicious when served with her Caesar-Like Salad with Croutons (page 15). We hope you will find in these pages your own favorites to use for countless good-neighbor occasions to come.

We look forward to hearing about your good-neighbor cooking experiences at www.thegoodneighborcookbook.com.

CHAPTER 1

BRINGING HOME BABY

NEW Baby!

Snacks
- Cranberry Granola Bars
- Fresh Fruit and Yogurt Cups
- Three Smoothie Kits
- Two Surprise Sandwiches
- Really Good Biscuits

Salads
- Lemony Potato and Fennel Salad with Arugula
- Orzo Salad with Tomatoes, Feta, and Dill
- Three Green Salads and Three Vinaigrettes

Soups
- Hearty Minestrone Soup with Potato Gnocchi
- Sweet Potato and Rice Soup
- Summer Tomato Gazpacho

Main Dishes
- Creamy Tomato Baked Ravioli and Spinach
- Sausage and Lentil Stew
- Big-Batch Bolognese
- Spring Vegetable Chicken Potpie
- Easy-Bake Eggplant Lasagne
- Chicken Two Ways

Sweet Treats
- Chocolate Pudding Pots
- Nectarine Crisp
- Chewy Gingersnaps
- Brown Butter Blueberry Muffins

A newborn is a joy and a blessing and, in terms of impact on a household, not unlike a tornado. Between round-the-clock feedings, diaper-change-a-thons, and mounting piles of laundry, new parents barely have time to grab a shower, let alone a nap. Assembling a potpie? It's not going to happen.

Yet now more than ever, Mom needs to stay nourished, especially if she is nursing. A woman's body will make milk production its top priority, so a breastfeeding woman who lives on fast food is not likely to jeopardize her baby's health. Still, a nursing mom powered by jelly doughnuts will compromise her own nutritional needs (and probably risk biting off her spouse's head!). If she eats healthfully, and often, she will have the stamina for 2 a.m. feedings, plus the emotional wherewithal to stay calm when the baby starts wailing at the exact moment the FedEx guy arrives.

That's where this chapter comes in. Mom will be thrilled when you turn up with high-energy snacks such as Cranberry Granola Bars (page 4) and Three Smoothie Kits (page 6), or fixings for inventive sandwiches that she'd never make for herself, like Turkey, Brie, and Apple Baguette (page 8). This chapter also includes one-dish main courses, such as Sausage and Lentil Stew (page 22) and Easy-Bake Eggplant Lasagne (page 26), which yields enough servings to feed the whole family—not just today but also tomorrow.

A variety of flavors is also a big bonus if Mom is breastfeeding. Studies have found that breast milk is flavored by the foods the mother eats, so infants exposed to an array of tastes tend to be less picky eaters later in life. That's a great reason to drop off Summer Tomato Gazpacho (page 20). Families of newborns always appreciate a complete meal, so choose among the fresh green salads and vinaigrettes in this chapter, and pick up a fresh loaf of bread from the bakery. Even better, consider organizing a meal train for the family (see page 19).

You may want to wait a few weeks to bring over your cooking. Often, there's an onslaught of food deliveries during the baby's first week; but when she is six weeks old and no longer sleeping 20 hours a day, the family may be even more desperate for your Big-Batch Bolognese (page 23).

Cranberry Granola Bars

Prep time: 10 minutes
Total time: 2 hours 55 minutes (includes cooling time)
Makes 20 bars

These homemade energy bars are the perfect eat-one-handed-while-holding-the-baby snack. Mom can keep a stash of these in the bedroom for a boost 'round the clock. Break up a bar over yogurt and you have a creamy, crumbly, calcium-rich breakfast; do the same over ice cream and there you go: a scrumptious dessert.

2 cups old-fashioned rolled oats

1 cup sliced almonds

1 cup sweetened flaked coconut

¼ cup unsalted sunflower seeds

2 tablespoons sesame seeds

¾ cup pure maple syrup

⅓ cup firmly packed dark brown sugar

2 tablespoons olive oil

¼ teaspoon kosher salt

1 cup dried cranberries

Preheat the oven to 350°F. Lightly oil a 9 by 13-inch baking pan. Line the bottom of the pan with parchment paper, leaving a 2-inch overhang on two sides.

Spread the oats, almonds, coconut, sunflower seeds, and sesame seeds on a rimmed baking sheet. Bake, stirring once, until lightly golden, 12 to 15 minutes.

Decrease the oven temperature to 300°F.

Meanwhile, in a large bowl, combine the syrup, sugar, oil, and salt, stirring until the sugar dissolves. Add the toasted oat mixture and cranberries and stir to coat. Scrape the mixture into the prepared pan, firmly pressing down in an even layer with a rubber spatula.

Transfer the pan to the oven and bake until golden brown and set, 25 to 30 minutes.

Let cool completely on a wire rack, at least 2 hours. Grabbing the ends of the parchment, lift out the granola and slice into bars. Store in an airtight container for up to 5 days.

Fresh Fruit and Yogurt Cups

Prep time: 5 minutes
Total time: 5 minutes
Serves 8

Fruit and yogurt, like sandwiches, always taste better when someone else has prepared them for you.

4 cups plain Greek or other thick yogurt

1 pint fresh berries (such as blueberries, raspberries, or sliced strawberries)

¼ cup honey

Divide the yogurt and berries among 8 (8-ounce) disposable cups and drizzle with the honey. Wrap tightly with plastic wrap, and refrigerate for up to 5 days.

COOK'S TIP: Place the cups in an 8-inch square baking pan for delivery, and transfer the cups to the refrigerator upon arrival. These yogurt cups are a wonderful companion to the Cranberry Granola Bars on page 4.

Three Smoothie Kits

With smoothie kits in the freezer, an exhausted new parent is seconds away from a nutritious, creamy meal-in-a-glass. The ingredients are all prepped, measured, and frozen. Just add yogurt and a little milk or juice, and blend. Be sure to write on each bag how much yogurt and milk or juice to add.

Peanut Butter, Banana, and Honey Smoothie

Prep time: 5 minutes
Total time: 5 minutes
Makes 4 kits; 2 servings each

8 ripe bananas, sliced
1 cup smooth peanut butter
¼ cup honey
1 quart milk
2 cups plain yogurt

Divide the bananas, peanut butter, and honey among four 1-quart resealable plastic bags and freeze overnight. For each kit, puree in the blender with 1 cup of the milk and ½ cup of the yogurt.

Mixed Berry and Banana Smoothie

Prep time: 5 minutes
Total time: 5 minutes
Makes 4 kits; 2 servings each

4 cups fresh or frozen blueberries
4 cups fresh or frozen strawberries
4 bananas, sliced
1 quart fresh orange juice
2 cups plain yogurt

Divide the blueberries, strawberries, and bananas among four 1-quart resealable plastic bags and freeze overnight. For each kit, puree in the blender with 1 cup of the juice and ½ cup of the yogurt.

Raspberry-Peach Smoothie

Prep time: 5 minutes
Total time: 5 minutes
Makes 4 kits; 2 servings each

4 cups fresh or frozen raspberries

4 cups fresh or frozen sliced peaches

1 cup raspberry sorbet

1 quart pineapple juice

2 cups plain yogurt

Divide the raspberries, peaches, and sorbet among four 1-quart resealable plastic bags and freeze overnight. For each kit, puree in the blender with 1 cup of the pineapple juice and ½ cup of the yogurt.

COOK'S TIP: The liquid measurement for each recipe is based on using a frozen packet. If you decide to make the smoothies without freezing the packet beforehand, add about 1 cup of ice per packet to the blender. Also, the smoothies will need less milk or juice, so add it a little at a time.

Two Surprise Sandwiches

These perky sandwiches—one turkey, one vegetarian—will make a hungry new mama smile.

Turkey, Brie, and Apple Baguette

Prep time: 10 minutes
Total time: 10 minutes
Serves 4

1 baguette (about 20 inches)

3 tablespoons Dijon mustard

8 ounces thinly sliced turkey breast

1 small bunch arugula

1 apple, thinly sliced, such as Granny Smith or Golden Delicious

8 ounces Brie cheese, sliced

Slice the baguette in half horizontally. Spread the mustard over the bottom half, then layer with the turkey, arugula, apple, and Brie. Top with the top half of the bread and cut the baguette into 4 sandwiches (or more for smaller sandwiches). Wrap tightly with waxed paper or plastic wrap.

Cucumber, Celery, Sprout, and Cream Cheese Sandwich

Prep time: 10 minutes
Total time: 10 minutes
Serves 4

8 slices whole-grain bread

4 ounces cream cheese

1 rib celery, thinly sliced

2 Kirby cucumbers, thinly sliced

2 medium beefsteak tomatoes, thinly sliced

1 cup fresh sprouts, such as alfalfa or radish

Pinch of kosher salt and freshly ground black pepper

Spread each slice of bread with the cream cheese. Layer 4 of the slices of bread with the celery, cucumbers, tomatoes, and sprouts. Sprinkle with the salt and pepper and top with the remaining 4 slices of bread. Wrap tightly with waxed paper or plastic wrap.

Really Good Biscuits

Prep time: 10 minutes
Total time: 25 minutes
Makes 10 biscuits

This down-home recipe is a reminder of just how good biscuits really are. No need for a mix; odds are, you already have the ingredients in your pantry. The biscuits are "really good" cold, but if Mom finds herself with an extra moment, she can add a slice of ham or try one warmed with butter and a drizzle of honey.

2 cups all-purpose flour, spooned and leveled

2 teaspoons baking powder

1 teaspoon sugar

½ teaspoon kosher salt

6 tablespoons (¾ stick) cold unsalted butter, cut into small pieces

¾ cup whole milk

Preheat the oven to 425°F. Line a baking sheet with parchment paper.

In a large bowl, whisk together the flour, baking powder, sugar, and salt. Using a pastry blender or your fingers, cut in the butter until coarse, irregular crumbs form.

Stir in the milk until just combined.

Turn the dough onto a floured surface and knead twice to bring it together. Shape and pat it into a ¾-inch-thick disk. Using a 2-inch round biscuit cutter (or drinking glass), cut the biscuits, reshaping and cutting the scraps as necessary. Transfer to the prepared baking sheet and bake until light golden brown, 10 to 12 minutes. Let cool on a wire rack.

COOK'S TIP: These biscuits cook beautifully directly from the freezer in 12 to 15 minutes. Make a double batch of dough: Deliver one batch already baked and the other unbaked and tightly wrapped with plastic wrap and aluminum foil for the freezer (freeze for up to 1 month). Don't forget to include the simple baking instructions for the frozen batch.

Lemony Potato and Fennel Salad with Arugula

Prep time: 15 minutes
Total time: 25 minutes
Serves 6 to 8

Deliver this fresh, flavorful potato salad with a package of baby arugula. Toss in the greens as needed to transform this side dish into a hearty supper salad.

2½ pounds baby red potatoes

⅓ cup sour cream

¼ cup freshly squeezed lemon juice (from 2 lemons)

1 teaspoon kosher salt

¼ teaspoon freshly ground black pepper

1 medium fennel bulb, halved and thinly sliced

1 cup loosely packed fresh flat-leaf parsley, coarsely chopped

6 cups baby arugula, for serving

Place the potatoes in a large pot, cover with cold water, and bring to a boil. Add a large pinch of salt, decrease the heat, and simmer until the potatoes are tender when pierced with a paring knife, 15 to 18 minutes. Drain and run under cold water to cool, then cut into quarters.

In a large bowl, whisk together the sour cream, lemon juice, salt, and pepper. Stir in the fennel, parsley, and potatoes. Refrigerate in an airtight container for up to 4 days. Just before serving, toss the salad with the arugula.

Orzo Salad with Tomatoes, Feta, and Dill

Prep time: 15 minutes
Total time: 25 minutes
Serves 6 to 8

This pasta salad is loaded with the fresh flavors of the Mediterranean. It's substantial enough for a light meal and perfect for an emergency snack.

1 pound orzo

1 pint grape or cherry tomatoes, halved

1 cup pitted Kalamata olives, halved

1 small red onion, chopped

¾ cup loosely packed fresh dill, chopped

¼ cup extra-virgin olive oil

2 tablespoons red wine vinegar

¾ teaspoon kosher salt

¼ teaspoon freshly ground black pepper

1 cup (4 ounces) crumbled feta cheese

Cook the orzo according to the package directions; drain and run under cold water to cool.

Meanwhile, in a large bowl, combine the tomatoes, olives, onion, dill, oil, vinegar, salt, and pepper. Add the orzo and toss well. Gently fold in the feta.

Refrigerate in an airtight container for up to 4 days.

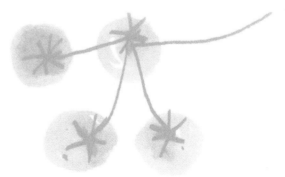

Three Green Salads and Three Vinaigrettes

Salads are often an afterthought, but when you toss in just the right ingredients, a green salad can be the most memorable part of the meal. These three simple, fresh salad recipes and eclectic variations, along with perfectly paired vinaigrettes, give salads their due.

Butter Lettuce Salad with Toasted Pine Nuts, Herbs, and Citrus Vinaigrette

Prep time: 15 minutes
Total time: 15 minutes

Serves 4

¼ cup pine nuts

2 heads butter lettuce, torn into bite-size pieces

1 cup loosely packed fresh flat-leaf parsley, coarsely chopped

¼ cup chopped fresh chives

4 to 5 tablespoons Citrus Vinaigrette (recipe follows)

Place the pine nuts in a small dry skillet over medium heat and cook, tossing, until light golden brown, 3 to 4 minutes. Transfer to a bowl to cool.

In a large bowl, toss the lettuce, parsley, chives, pine nuts, and the vinaigrette.

COOK'S TIP: For variations on this salad, add a sectioned grapefruit and a diced avocado or a pint of halved cherry tomatoes and 4 ounces of diced fresh mozzarella cheese.

Citrus Vinaigrette

Makes about 1¹/₃ cups

1 shallot, chopped

1 tablespoon honey

1 teaspoon Dijon mustard

½ cup freshly squeezed orange juice (from about 2 oranges)

¼ cup white wine vinegar

¹/³ cup extra-virgin olive oil

½ teaspoon kosher salt

¼ teaspoon freshly ground black pepper

In a medium bowl, whisk together the shallot, honey, mustard, orange juice, vinegar, oil, salt, and pepper.

COOK'S TIP: This is enough vinaigrette for four or five salads. Refrigerate in an airtight container for up to 2 weeks.

Arugula, Radish, Cucumber, and Olive Salad with Balsamic Vinaigrette

Prep time: 15 minutes

Total time: 15 minutes

Serves 4

2 bunches arugula (8 cups), stemmed

2 scallions (white and light green parts), chopped

4 radishes, thinly sliced

1 Kirby cucumber, quartered lengthwise and sliced

¼ cup Kalamata or oil-cured black olives, pitted

4 to 5 tablespoons Balsamic Vinaigrette (recipe follows)

In a large bowl, toss the arugula, scallions, radishes, cucumber, olives, and the vinaigrette.

COOK'S TIP: For variations on this salad, instead of the radishes, cucumber, and olives, substitute a sliced fresh nectarine or apple, ¼ chopped roasted almonds, and ½ cup crumbled blue cheese. Or instead of the radishes, cucumber, and olives, substitute ¼ cup chopped roasted walnuts, 4 slices cooked and crumbled bacon, and ¼ cup crumbled Parmesan cheese.

Balsamic Vinaigrette

Makes about 1½ cups

2 teaspoons Dijon mustard

½ cup balsamic vinegar

1 cup extra-virgin olive oil

1 teaspoon kosher salt

¼ teaspoon freshly ground black pepper

In a medium bowl, whisk together the mustard, vinegar, oil, salt, and pepper.

COOK'S TIP: If you prefer red wine vinegar to balsamic vinegar, substitute one for the other. This is enough vinaigrette for five or six salads. Store in an airtight container for up to 1 month.

Caesar-Like Salad with Croutons

Prep time: 15 minutes

Total time: 20 minutes

Serves 4

4 cups 1-inch fresh bread cubes, from a baguette or French bread

3 tablespoons olive oil

½ teaspoon kosher salt

8 cups chopped romaine lettuce (from 1 to 2 heads)

5 to 6 tablespoons Caesar-Like Vinaigrette (recipe follows)

Preheat the oven to 375°F.

On a baking sheet, toss together the bread cubes, oil, and salt.

Bake, stirring once, until golden and crisp, 12 to 15 minutes.

In a large bowl, toss the lettuce, 1 cup of the croutons, and the vinaigrette.

COOK'S TIP: This recipe leaves you with croutons to spare for other salads. To add variety to this salad, add thinly sliced fennel and parsley leaves to the romaine and croutons, or add a sliced Kirby cucumber and 2 chopped hard-boiled eggs to the romaine and croutons.

Caesar-Like Vinaigrette

Makes about 1⅓ cups

2 cloves garlic, minced

¼ cup freshly squeezed lemon
    juice (from about 2 lemons)

2 tablespoons grated Parmesan
    cheese

2 tablespoons Dijon mustard

2 teaspoons Worcestershire sauce

Dash of hot sauce, such as
    Tabasco

1 cup olive oil

¾ teaspoon kosher salt

¼ teaspoon freshly ground
    black pepper

In a medium bowl, whisk together the garlic, lemon juice, Parmesan, mustard, Worcestershire, and hot sauce. While whisking, slowly add the oil. Season with the salt and pepper.

COOK'S TIP: This is enough vinaigrette for four or five salads. Refrigerate in an airtight container for up to 1 week.

Hearty Minestrone Soup with Potato Gnocchi

Prep time: 15 minutes
Total time: 40 minutes
Serves 6 to 8

Nothing nourishes a frazzled family like a big pot of minestrone soup. Potato gnocchi—small, quick-cooking dumplings found in the fresh or dried pasta section in supermarkets—make the soup even more satisfying. Deliver this Italian favorite with a loaf of bread and the Caesar-Like Salad (page 15).

2 tablespoons olive oil

1 medium yellow onion, chopped

4 ribs celery, thinly sliced

4 medium carrots, peeled, halved lengthwise, and sliced

½ teaspoon kosher salt

1 (14.5-ounce) can diced tomatoes with juice

2 (15.5-ounce) cans kidney beans, rinsed and drained

½ head savoy or green cabbage, halved and thinly sliced (about 6 cups)

6 cups low-sodium chicken broth

1 pound store-bought potato gnocchi

1 cup fresh flat-leaf parsley, chopped

Grated Parmesan cheese, for serving

Heat the oil in a large saucepan over medium-high heat. Add the onion, celery, carrots, and salt and cook, stirring often, until tender, about 10 minutes (decrease the heat, as necessary, to prevent scorching). Add the tomatoes and cook, stirring, for 5 minutes more. Stir in the beans, cabbage, and broth and bring to a boil. Decrease the heat and simmer until the cabbage is tender, about 10 minutes.

Add the gnocchi and simmer until they are cooked through and tender, 3 to 4 minutes. Stir in the parsley and serve with Parmesan.

COOK'S TIP: This is a great recipe to double—one batch to eat now, one to freeze for later. Refrigerate in an airtight container for up to 4 days or freeze for up to 2 months.

Sweet Potato and Rice Soup

Prep time: 15 minutes
Total time: 45 minutes
Serves 6 to 8

This hearty soup warms you through and through and is prepared with a wonderfully minimal ingredients list. Look for the garnet type of sweet potato, with its dark purple skin and bright orange flesh.

2 tablespoons olive oil

1 medium yellow onion, chopped

4 ribs celery, thinly sliced

½ teaspoon kosher salt

2 pounds sweet potatoes (about 4 medium), peeled and cut into ½-inch pieces

8 cups low-sodium chicken broth

1 cup long-grain white rice

2 teaspoons fresh thyme leaves

¼ teaspoon freshly ground black pepper

Heat the oil in a large saucepan over medium-high heat. Add the onion, celery, and salt and cook, stirring often, until tender, about 10 minutes (decrease the heat, as necessary, to prevent scorching). Add the potatoes and cook, stirring, for 3 minutes more. Add the broth, rice, thyme, and pepper and bring to a boil. Decrease the heat and simmer until the rice is tender, 15 to 20 minutes.

COOK'S TIP: Rice absorbs liquid as it sits, so upon reheating, you may have to add a bit of water or chicken broth to reach your desired consistency. Refrigerate this soup in an airtight container for up to 4 days or freeze for up to 2 months.

How to Organize
a Meal Train

One of the best ways to help parents of a newborn is to serve as the family's meal scheduler and leave the cooking to others. Meal trains also can be a godsend for families coping with illness or death. Here's what to keep in mind.

• Ask if new parents prefer to have meals delivered daily, twice a week, or weekly. Or, they may prefer a "frozen meal train": To minimize interruptions, friends deliver frozen or freezable dishes on a single day. The family may want to leave a cooler on the porch with a big "Thank you!" note. Meal-train participants should put their names on their containers, along with the date, the name of the dish, and heating instructions.

• Ask if any family members have food allergies or special preferences, so that you don't end up bringing a pot roast to a family of vegetarians.

• Use a free online invitation service such as Evite.com. Gather the e-mail addresses of the meal-train participants, and send an Evite indicating the family's needs and requested delivery dates. Evite allows contributors to sign up for specific dates and to post messages indicating their planned dish, so that the family doesn't end up with six chicken casseroles. Include the family's phone number on the Evite in case of last-minute emergencies. You don't want them waiting for a meal that isn't going to arrive.

• Consider the kids. If the new baby has older siblings, package your meal with foods that most kids, even picky ones, will eat, such as cut-up apples, melon, and other fruits; dipping fruit in yogurt is always fun for kids. Many children also go for cut-up veggies, such as baby carrots, red peppers, and cucumbers, and hummus makes for a yummy veggie dip. Generally, any dish with pasta goes over well with children. It's best to leave sauces on the side.

Summer Tomato Gazpacho

Prep time: 15 minutes
Total time: 15 minutes
Serves 4 to 6

When even turning on the stove seems too big a task, zesty, chunky gazpacho is your best friend: no heating necessary. Packed with vitamins and bursting with flavor, this soup goes perfectly with a loaf of crusty fresh bread. If you're in the mood for additions, stir in fresh corn kernels and top with a dollop of sour cream and some diced avocado.

3 medium red bell peppers (about 12 ounces), cored

2 regular cucumbers (about 1 pound), peeled and seeded

2½ pounds ripe beefsteak tomatoes, cored and cut into chunks

2 cloves garlic

3 tablespoons sherry or red wine vinegar

2 tablespoons extra-virgin olive oil

1½ teaspoons kosher salt

¼ teaspoon freshly ground black pepper

Cut 2 of the red peppers and 1 of the cucumbers into large pieces and place in a blender. Add the tomatoes, garlic, vinegar, oil, salt, pepper, and ½ cup water and puree until smooth (you may have to do this in batches). Cut the remaining bell pepper and cucumber into ¼-inch pieces and stir into the soup. Serve well chilled.

Refrigerate in an airtight container for up to 4 days or freeze for up to 2 months.

Creamy Tomato Baked Ravioli and Spinach

Prep time: 10 minutes
Total time: 35 minutes
Serves 6 to 8

This 10-minute-prep casserole with fresh cheese ravioli will quickly become a household staple—kids love it. For variety, try butternut squash or mushroom ravioli. The casserole goes well with Caesar-Like Salad (page 15).

3 cups Toasted Garlic Marinara (page 65) or 1 (24-ounce) jar store-bought marinara

1 cup heavy cream

2 pounds fresh store-bought cheese ravioli (from the refrigerator section)

4 cups baby spinach

16 fresh basil leaves, torn

¼ cup (1 ounce) grated Parmesan cheese

Preheat the oven to 400°F.

In a large bowl, combine the marinara and cream. Stir in the uncooked ravioli, spinach, and basil until well coated. Transfer to a 2½- to 3-quart casserole dish and sprinkle with the Parmesan. Bake until the sauce is bubbling and the top is golden, 20 to 25 minutes.

COOK'S TIP: Assemble the dish up to 24 hours in advance and deliver it, unbaked, with the easy baking directions included.

Sausage and Lentil Stew

Prep time: 15 minutes
Total time: 1 hour 10 minutes
Serves 4

This humble, veggie-rich stew will satisfy the hungriest of new moms. Lentils are rich in low-fat protein and fiber and are among the best vegetarian sources of iron and folate. Make this a year-round favorite by substituting kale for chard in the cold winter months.

2 tablespoons olive oil

1½ pounds sweet Italian sausage (8 small links)

1 medium yellow onion, chopped

2 medium carrots, peeled and cut into ½-inch pieces

2 cloves garlic, chopped

1 (15-ounce) can diced tomatoes with juice

1 cup green lentils (preferably French lentils de Puy)

1 small bunch Swiss chard, cut crosswise into 1-inch strips

1 tablespoon fresh thyme leaves

½ teaspoon kosher salt

¼ teaspoon freshly ground black pepper

Heat 1 tablespoon of the oil in a large saucepan over medium-high heat. Cook the sausages until browned and cooked through, 6 to 8 minutes; transfer to a plate. Pour off any drippings left in the pan.

Heat the remaining 1 tablespoon oil in the same saucepan. Add the onion and carrots and cook, stirring often, until tender, 8 to 10 minutes (decrease the heat, as necessary, to prevent scorching). Stir in the garlic and cook for 1 minute, then add the tomatoes and cook, stirring, for 3 to 4 minutes. Add the lentils, chard, thyme, salt, pepper, and 2 cups water and bring to a boil. Nestle in the sausages, decrease the heat, and simmer, covered, until the lentils are tender, 25 to 30 minutes.

COOK'S TIP: French lentils de Puy are uniquely nutty and hold their shape when cooked, so if you see them in the market, opt for these special lentils. Otherwise, regular green lentils are perfectly fine. Keep them on hand for a quick-cooking side or for cool salads simply dressed with a mustard vinaigrette and tossed with red onion and fresh herbs.

Big-Batch Bolognese

Prep time: 25 minutes
Total time: 55 minutes
Serves 8

A sleep-deprived family living on takeout and bottled sauces will be indebted when this fresh, meaty, garlicky sauce arrives. It's perfect for fettuccine or rigatoni and works well for a lasagne filling, too. Make a double batch and freeze half for yourself; it'll come in handy the next time you need to whip up a meal in a pinch.

2 tablespoons olive oil

2 medium yellow onions, finely chopped

2 medium carrots, finely chopped

2 ribs celery, finely chopped

4 cloves garlic, finely chopped

2 teaspoons kosher salt

1 pound ground beef chuck

1 pound ground pork

1 (6-ounce) can tomato paste

1 cup dry white wine

1 cup whole or low-fat milk

½ teaspoon crushed red pepper

¼ teaspoon freshly ground black pepper

1 bay leaf

Pinch of freshly grated nutmeg

Heat the oil in a large pot over medium-high heat. Add the onions, carrots, celery, garlic, and ½ teaspoon of the salt and cook, stirring often, until the vegetables are very tender, about 15 minutes (decrease the heat, as necessary, to prevent scorching).

With the heat still on medium-high, add the beef and pork to the pot and cook, breaking up with a spoon, until no longer pink, 6 to 8 minutes. Add the tomato paste and cook, stirring, for 3 minutes more. Add the wine, milk, 2 cups water, crushed red pepper, black pepper, bay leaf, nutmeg, and the remaining 1½ teaspoons salt and bring to a boil.

Decrease the heat and simmer, stirring occasionally, until the sauce has thickened and the flavors have developed, about 30 minutes.

COOK'S TIP: If you're not a lover of pork, simply double the amount of beef. Ground turkey also works beautifully here in place of both the beef and pork. Refrigerate the sauce in an airtight container for up to 4 days or freeze for up to 2 months.

Spring Vegetable Chicken Potpie

Prep time: 45 minutes
Total time: 1 hour 45 minutes
Serves 4 to 6

Nothing is more satisfying than a chicken potpie, with its flaky top and succulent filling. This updated version has a puff pastry top and an all-breast-meat filling spiked with vegetables and fresh herbs. It's not the quickest recipe in the book, to be sure, but it's well worth the effort. If you're in a hurry, using a rotisserie chicken is a great time-saver.

4 bone-in chicken breast halves (about 3 pounds)

8 cups low-sodium chicken broth

3 tablespoons olive oil

4 leeks (white and light green parts), halved lengthwise and sliced into half-moons

4 medium carrots, cut into ½-inch pieces

1 teaspoon kosher salt

¼ cup all-purpose flour, spooned and leveled

½ cup dry white wine

1½ cups frozen peas

1 cup loosely packed fresh flat-leaf parsley, chopped

1 tablespoon chopped fresh tarragon

¼ teaspoon freshly ground black pepper

1 sheet frozen puff pastry (from a 17.25-ounce package), thawed

Place the chicken and enough chicken broth to cover (adding water, if necessary) in a large pot and bring to a boil. Decrease the heat and gently simmer until the chicken is cooked through, 20 to 25 minutes. Transfer the chicken to a bowl and, when cool enough to handle, shred into pieces. Reserve 2½ cups of the broth, and refrigerate or freeze the rest of the broth for another use.

Meanwhile, heat the oven to 375°F.

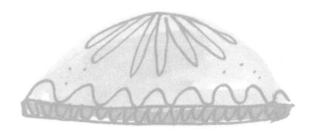

Heat the oil in a large pot over medium-high heat. Add the leeks, carrots, and ½ teaspoon of the salt and cook, stirring often, until beginning to soften, 8 to 10 minutes (decrease the heat, as necessary, to prevent scorching). Stir in the flour and cook for 1 minute. Gradually stir in the wine and 2½ cups of the reserved chicken broth and bring to a boil. Add the peas, parsley, tarragon, pepper, chicken, and the remaining ½ teaspoon salt.

Transfer to an 8-inch square (1½-quart) baking dish. Place the puff pastry over the top of the chicken and vegetables, letting it hang over the sides of the dish, and cut vents in the top. Place the dish on a rimmed baking sheet and bake until the top is golden brown and crisp, 35 to 40 minutes.

COOK'S TIP: You can make the filling up to a day in advance, transfer it to the baking dish, and refrigerate. When ready to bake, top with the puff pastry, and then bake according to recipe instructions, adding 5 to 10 minutes to the cooking time.

Easy-Bake Eggplant Lasagne

Prep time: 1 hour
Total time: 1 hour 15 minutes
Serves 8

The eggplant in this scrumptious and substantial meatless main dish is baked rather than fried—you get all the flavor without the guilt. The lasagne makes for wonderful leftovers and freezes well for up to 2 months.

½ cup plus 2 tablespoons olive oil

2 medium yellow onions, thinly sliced

4 cloves garlic, finely chopped

2 teaspoons kosher salt

2 (28-ounce) cans whole peeled tomatoes with juice

2 teaspoons dried oregano

1 teaspoon sugar

½ teaspoon crushed red pepper

¼ teaspoon freshly ground black pepper

2½ cups dried bread crumbs

½ cup all-purpose flour, spooned and leveled

4 large eggs, beaten

1 large eggplant, cut into ¼-inch-thick rounds

1½ cups (6 ounces) grated mozzarella cheese

1½ cups (6 ounces) grated Gruyère cheese

¼ cup (2 ounces) grated Parmesan cheese

Preheat the oven to 400°F.

Heat 2 tablespoons of the oil in a large pot over medium-high heat. Add the onions, garlic, and ½ teaspoon of the salt and cook, stirring often, until softened and light golden brown, 10 to 12 minutes (decrease the heat, as necessary, to prevent scorching). Add the tomatoes, oregano, sugar, crushed red pepper, black pepper, and ½ teaspoon of the salt and simmer, breaking up the tomatoes with a spoon, until slightly thickened, about 20 minutes.

Meanwhile, in a medium bowl, combine the bread crumbs, the remaining ½ cup oil, and the remaining 1 teaspoon salt. Place the flour and eggs in separate bowls. Dip the eggplant slices first into the flour, then into the eggs, and finally into the bread crumb mixture, pressing to help them adhere. Arrange in an even layer on 2 baking sheets and bake until tender and crispy, 12 to 15 minutes.

In a 9 by 13-inch baking pan, spread 1½ cups of the sauce over the bottom. Layer half of the eggplant over the sauce, then add another 1½ cups of sauce. Sprinkle with half of each cheese. Repeat with the remaining eggplant, sauce, and cheeses. Bake until heated through and bubbling, 15 to 20 minutes.

COOK'S TIP: Refrigerate, tightly wrapped, for up to 4 days. To reheat, cover with aluminum foil and bake at 400°F until heated through, about 30 minutes. Freeze, unbaked and tightly wrapped with foil, for up to 2 months. Bake directly from the freezer, covered, for about 1 hour.

Chicken Two Ways

Prep time: 25 minutes
Total time: 1 hour 10 minutes
Makes 2 dinners; 4 servings each

Roast one chicken and you can provide two completely different dinners: burritos for the first night and Asian chicken salad for the next. With simple assembly required, meal kits are great for families with older kids—they're a good way to let them pitch in and feel helpful.

1 (4-pound) chicken
1 tablespoon olive oil
¾ teaspoon kosher salt
¼ teaspoon freshly ground
 black pepper

Preheat the oven to 400°F.

Place the chicken in a roasting pan, rub with the oil, and season with the salt and pepper. Roast until cooked through, 50 to 60 minutes. Let cool, then shred the meat and divide between 2 resealable plastic bags.

Burrito Dinner Kit

1 head romaine lettuce,
 thinly sliced
2 cups (8 ounces) grated
 Monterey Jack cheese
1 (15.5-ounce) can pinto or black
 beans
1 (16-ounce container) store-
 bought fresh salsa
1 (8-ounce container) sour cream
8 (10-inch) flour tortillas

Place the lettuce and cheese in separate resealable plastic bags and deliver along with the beans, salsa, sour cream, and tortillas.

Include serving instructions: Heat 1 cup of the salsa in a skillet over medium heat. Stir in 1 bag of the chicken and the beans (rinse and drain them first) and cook until heated through. Warm the tortillas and assemble the burritos with the chicken mixture, lettuce, cheese, sour cream, and the remaining salsa.

Asian Chicken Salad Kit

1 head romaine lettuce, thinly sliced

2 Kirby cucumbers, quartered lengthwise and thinly sliced

1 red bell pepper, cored and thinly sliced

1 cup loosely packed fresh cilantro, chopped

4 scallions (white and light green parts), thinly sliced

1 (8-ounce can) water chestnuts, drained and coarsely chopped

½ cup cashews, coarsely chopped

3 tablespoons rice vinegar

3 tablespoons canola oil

1½ teaspoons low-sodium soy sauce

¾ teaspoon sugar

In a large resealable plastic bag, combine the lettuce, cucumbers, bell pepper, cilantro, scallions, and water chestnuts. Place the cashews in a separate bag.

In a small container with a tight-fitting lid, combine the vinegar, oil, soy sauce, and sugar.

Include serving instructions: Toss the salad mixture and cashews with the vinaigrette.

COOK'S TIP: In a pinch, you can use rotisserie chicken from your grocery deli, but quite often they weigh no more than 2½ pounds, so you may have to buy two.

Chocolate Pudding Pots

Prep time: 20 minutes
Total time: 6 hours 20 minutes (includes cooling time)
Serves 8

What is more splendid than homemade chocolate pudding? And when was the last time you had some? Use disposable cups to deliver these old-fashioned treats. They're not just for kids!

¾ cup sugar

5 tablespoons cornstarch

¼ cup unsweetened cocoa powder

¼ teaspoon kosher salt

4 cups whole milk

4 large egg yolks

4 ounces semisweet chocolate, chopped

2 tablespoons unsalted butter

1 teaspoon pure vanilla extract

In a medium saucepan, whisk together the sugar, cornstarch, cocoa powder, and salt. Gradually whisk in the milk, then the egg yolks. Cook, stirring constantly with a wooden spoon, over medium heat until thickened (you don't want it to boil). The pudding will continue to thicken as it cools.

Remove from the heat and add the chocolate, butter, and vanilla and whisk until melted and smooth. Divide among 8 (6-ounce) cups, wrap tightly with plastic wrap, and refrigerate until chilled, 6 hours or overnight.

COOK'S TIP: If small lumps appear in your pudding, it means the eggs have curdled. If this happens, strain the mixture through a fine-mesh sieve before adding the chocolate, butter, and vanilla.

Nectarine Crisp

Prep time: 20 minutes
Total time: 1 hour 10 minutes
Serves 8

A crisp, crumbly topping blanketing summer's sweet nectarines, this is one of those desserts you secretly keep spooning from the fridge. You can use this irresistible topping with any fruit or fruit combination, such as apples and blackberries or peaches and blueberries.

4 pounds nectarines (about 10), cut into wedges

⅓ cup granulated sugar

1 cup firmly packed dark brown sugar

¾ cup all-purpose flour, spooned and leveled

½ cup old-fashioned rolled oats

½ teaspoon kosher salt

¼ teaspoon ground cinnamon

½ cup (1 stick) cold unsalted butter, cut into small pieces

Preheat the oven to 400°F.

In a large bowl, toss together the nectarines and granulated sugar. Transfer to a 9 by 13-inch baking dish.

In the same bowl, combine the brown sugar, flour, oats, salt, and cinnamon. Using a pastry blender or your fingers, cut in the butter until crumbly. Pinch the crisp mixture into small clumps and sprinkle over the nectarines. Bake until the topping is crisp and the fruit is bubbling, 45 to 50 minutes. Let cool on a wire rack. Serve warm or at room temperature.

COOK'S TIP: Make a double batch of the crisp topping and keep it in an airtight container in the refrigerator for up to 2 weeks or in the freezer for up to 1 month. The next crisp you make will take no time at all.

Chewy Gingersnaps

Prep time: 20 minutes
Total time: 45 minutes
Makes 28 cookies

Having cookies on hand brightens anyone's mood. The molasses in this recipe enhances the gingersnaps' irresistible chewy texture. They're a fun alternative to plain old chocolate chip cookies (not that anyone minds those).

1½ cups all-purpose flour, spooned and leveled

¾ teaspoon baking soda

½ teaspoon ground cinnamon

½ teaspoon kosher salt

¼ teaspoon ground cloves

½ cup (1 stick) unsalted butter, at room temperature

¾ cup firmly packed dark brown sugar

1 large egg

¼ cup unsulfured molasses

2 tablespoons finely chopped candied ginger

1 teaspoon grated lemon zest

¼ cup granulated sugar

Preheat the oven to 350°F. Line 2 baking sheets with parchment paper.

In a medium bowl, whisk together the flour, baking soda, cinnamon, salt, and cloves.

Working with a stand mixer, preferably fitted with the paddle attachment, or with a hand mixer with a large bowl, beat the butter and brown sugar on medium speed until fluffy. Beat in the egg, then the molasses, ginger, and lemon zest. With the mixer on low speed, gradually mix in the flour mixture until just combined.

Refrigerate the dough for 20 minutes.

Shape the dough into tablespoon-size balls, then roll them in the granulated sugar to coat. Place 2 inches apart on the prepared baking sheets. Bake, rotating the sheets halfway through the baking time, until firm around the edges but still soft in the middle, 10 to 12 minutes. Let cool for 5 minutes on the baking sheets before transferring the cookies to wire racks.

COOK'S TIP: To ensure the cookies' chewiness, resist the urge to bake these gingersnaps any longer than 12 minutes. They will last in an airtight container for up to 3 days.

Brown Butter Blueberry Muffins

Prep time: 15 minutes
Total time: 35 minutes
Makes 12 muffins

The brown butter in this recipe adds a delectable nuttiness and richness to everyone's favorite muffin. These are great to have on hand for breakfast or an odd-hour pick-me-up.

2 cups all-purpose flour, spooned and leveled

½ cup plus 2 tablespoons sugar

2 teaspoons baking powder

½ teaspoon kosher salt

½ cup (1 stick) unsalted butter

1 cup whole milk

1 large egg, beaten

6 ounces (about 1½ cups) fresh blueberries

Preheat the oven to 400°F. Line a regular 12-cup muffin pan with paper liners or spray with nonstick cooking spray.

In a large bowl, whisk together the flour, ½ cup of the sugar, the baking powder, and salt and make a well in the center.

Melt the butter in a medium saucepan over medium heat. Once it is melted, swirl the pan until the butter begins to brown and smells beautifully nutty, 2 to 3 minutes. Remove from the heat.

Pour the butter, milk, and egg into the well of the flour and gently stir to combine (a few lumps in the batter are okay—do not overmix). Fold in the blueberries. Divide the batter evenly among the muffin cups and sprinkle the tops with the remaining 2 tablespoons sugar. Bake until a toothpick inserted into the center of a muffin comes out clean, 16 to 20 minutes. Let cool on wire racks before unmolding.

COOK'S TIP: Muffins freeze well. Wrap them individually in plastic wrap, then aluminum foil, and freeze for up to 1 month. Thaw in the refrigerator overnight.

CHAPTER 2

GET WELL SOON

Soups

- Chicken and Vegetable Soup with Lemon
- Sweet Potato, Parsnip, and Ginger Soup
- Asian Noodle Soup
- Beans and Greens Soup

Salads

- Chickpea and Cucumber Tabbouleh
- Quinoa-Walnut-Celery Salad

Main Dishes

- Turkey and Dill Meatloaf
- Roasted Cauliflower Macaroni and Cheese
- Chicken Cacciatore with Mashed Potatoes
- Rosemary Beef with Roasted Tomatoes and Potatoes
- Halibut, Leek, and Carrot Parchment Packets
- Stewed Chicken with Chickpeas and Lemon
- Zucchini and Parmesan Frittata

Sweet Treats

- Oat-Nut Scones
- Zucchini-Orange Bread
- Peanut Crunch Cookies

When a friend or relative is recuperating, nothing brings more cheer, or earns more appreciation, than a nutritious, homemade meal. Arriving at the door with a lovely soup, hearty main dish, and a sweet indulgence in hand is a gift to the whole family. Your friend will find sustenance in your Stewed Chicken with Chickpeas and Lemon (page 52), Turkey and Dill Meatloaf (page 45), and Oat-Nut Scones (page 55); her caregivers will be grateful for all the time and energy saved.

This chapter includes dishes to suit most any get-well situation, whether your recipient is undergoing extended cancer treatment or hobbling back from knee surgery. Some patients are instructed to load up on fiber, in which case a pot of Beans and Greens Soup (page 41) may be the best medicine. For those who need to limit roughage, Asian Noodle Soup (page 40) is just what the doctor ordered.

The dishes here are flavorful yet not overpowering—ideal for chemotherapy patients who have a diminished sense of taste and also are prone to nausea. No doubt convalescence is not the occasion for five-alarm chili or corned beef with sauerkraut! If the patient doesn't have much of an appetite, your gift will be feeding the family, so be sure to ask about their food preferences.

For this chapter, we have selected ingredients particularly rich in healing properties and immune-boosting nutrients—ginger, sweet potato, and bulgur wheat, to name a few. We also have kept the recipes on the lighter side, since people on the mend are less active than usual. Most of the dishes freeze well, so they can be enjoyed later.

Rest assured that your efforts will be cherished. A friend of ours whose husband recently underwent chemotherapy recalled that during those long months, she was exhausted, harried, and stumped for dinner ideas. "I hit bottom one day when I was at the checkout line with two impatient children, a box of wine, a pint of Ben & Jerry's, and two frozen kid's dinners. But the next day, a friend brought us dinner, and it felt like someone threw me a rope. I was so thankful."

Chicken and Vegetable Soup with Lemon

Prep time: 15 minutes
Total time: 1 hour 15 minutes
Serves 6 to 8

Nothing beats the subtle flavors of Mom's favorite cure-all. Enjoy this soup in its pure state, or let it be the starting point for your own creations: Add rice or pasta; seasonal vegetables such as peas, asparagus, Swiss chard, summer or winter squash; chopped fresh tomatoes; herbs and chopped garlic; or even freshly grated ginger.

1 (3½- to 4-pound chicken)

8 medium carrots (about 1½ pounds), peeled

4 ribs celery

1 medium yellow onion, quartered

2 teaspoons kosher salt

½ teaspoon black peppercorns

¼ cup freshly squeezed lemon juice (from about 2 lemons)

Place the chicken in a large pot. Cut 2 of the carrots and 2 of the celery ribs into 2-inch pieces and add to the pot along with the onion, salt, and peppercorns. Add enough cold water to cover (about 10 cups) and bring to a boil. Reduce the heat and simmer, skimming any foam that rises to the top, until the chicken is cooked through, about 45 minutes.

Transfer the chicken to a large bowl, and, when cool enough to handle, shred into bite-size pieces.

Meanwhile, strain the broth, discard the cooked vegetables, and return the broth to the pot. Thinly slice the remaining 6 carrots and 2 celery ribs and add them to the pot. Simmer until the vegetables are tender, about 10 minutes, and stir in the shredded chicken and lemon juice.

COOK'S TIP: When possible, look for chickens marked "organic." This ensures that they have been fed a hormone- and antibiotic-free diet. Refrigerate the soup in an airtight container for up to 4 days or freeze for up to 2 months.

Sweet Potato, Parsnip, and Ginger Soup

Prep time: 20 minutes
Total time: 45 minutes
Serves 6 to 8

The sweet potato–parsnip blend gives this velvety soup a hint of sweetness and a hefty dose of vitamins A and C, calcium, and potassium. Fresh ginger, known as a natural remedy for numerous ailments, adds a lemony warmth.

2 tablespoons olive oil

2 medium yellow onions, sliced

1 teaspoon kosher salt

2 pounds sweet potatoes (about 4 medium), peeled, halved, and sliced

8 ounces parsnips (about 2), peeled and sliced

6 cups low-sodium chicken broth, plus more if needed

1 tablespoon grated fresh ginger

¼ teaspoon freshly ground black pepper

Heat the oil in a large pot over medium-high heat. Add the onions and ½ teaspoon of the salt and cook, stirring often, until tender, about 10 minutes (decrease the heat, as necessary, to prevent scorching). Add the potatoes, parsnips, broth, ginger, pepper, and the remaining ½ teaspoon of salt and bring to a boil. Decrease the heat and simmer until the vegetables are tender, about 20 minutes.

Using a blender or an immersion blender, puree until smooth. Return the soup to the pot to reheat, adding more broth, if necessary, for the desired consistency.

COOK'S TIP: To freeze the soup, let it cool completely, then transfer to 1-quart resealable plastic bags and freeze them lying flat. This way you can stack them like books to economize on space. Using small bags allows you to thaw the soup quickly and without having to thaw more than you need. Freeze for up to 2 months or refrigerate for up to 4 days.

Asian Noodle Soup

Prep time: 10 minutes
Total time: 20 minutes
Serves 6 to 8

Asian noodle soup is said to have mystical healing powers. Who's to argue? Satisfying and soothing, this quick-to-prepare remedy is sure to calm the tenderest of stomachs. For a heartier version of this soup, substitute frozen, store-bought pot stickers or wontons for the noodles.

8 cups low-sodium chicken broth

3 tablespoons low-sodium soy sauce

1 teaspoon toasted sesame oil

6 thin carrots (about 1 pound), peeled and sliced into thin rounds

8 ounces Chinese noodles, such as wide lo mein, broken into pieces

4 ounces shiitake mushrooms, stemmed and thinly sliced

4 scallions (white and light green parts), thinly sliced

In a large saucepan, bring the chicken broth, soy sauce, and sesame oil to a boil. Add the carrots and noodles, lower the heat, and simmer until tender, 8 to 10 minutes. Stir in the mushrooms and scallions and simmer until the mushrooms are tender, about 5 minutes more. Refrigerate in an airtight container for up to 4 days.

Beans and Greens Soup

Prep time: 20 minutes
Total time: 30 minutes
Serves 6 to 8

Served alongside a thick slice of fresh bread, this fragrant, fiber-rich soup—loaded with potatoes, beans, and kale greens—is a meal in itself. The soup can easily be made vegetarian by substituting water for the chicken broth, though you may have to add a pinch more salt.

2 tablespoons olive oil

1 medium yellow onion, chopped

2 ribs celery, thinly sliced

4 cloves garlic, finely chopped

1 teaspoon kosher salt

8 cups low-sodium chicken broth

1 pound Yukon Gold or russet potatoes (about 2 medium), cut into ½-inch pieces

1 bunch kale, stemmed, and torn into small pieces (8 cups)

1 tablespoon chopped fresh rosemary

2 (15.5-ounce) cans cannellini beans, rinsed and drained

¼ cup (1 ounce) grated Parmesan cheese

½ teaspoon freshly ground black pepper

Heat the oil in a large pot over medium-high heat. Add the onion, celery, garlic, and ½ teaspoon of the salt and cook, stirring often, until softened, about 10 minutes. Add the chicken broth and bring to a boil. Add the potatoes, kale, rosemary, and the remaining ½ teaspoon salt and simmer until the vegetables are tender, about 15 minutes. Stir in the beans, Parmesan, and pepper and simmer to heat through.

Refrigerate in an airtight container for up to 4 days or freeze for up to 2 months.

Chickpea and Cucumber Tabbouleh

Prep time: 10 minutes
Total time: 30 minutes
Serves 6 to 8

Made from steamed, dried, cracked wheat, bulgur is perfect for cold salads because it maintains its texture without ever becoming soggy. The bulgur-chickpea combination makes this Mediterranean staple wonderfully filling—a great choice for vegetarians and omnivores alike. Serve the tabbouleh either alongside or stuffed into pita halves with our Hummus (page 87).

1½ cups bulgur wheat

3 cups hot water

4 scallions (white and light green parts), sliced

3 Kirby or 1 hothouse cucumber, quartered lengthwise and sliced

1 (15.5-ounce) can chickpeas, rinsed and drained

1½ cups loosely packed fresh flat-leaf parsley, chopped

½ cup loosely packed fresh mint leaves, chopped

¼ cup freshly squeezed lemon juice (from about 2 lemons)

3 tablespoons extra-virgin olive oil

1 teaspoon kosher salt

¼ teaspoon freshly ground black pepper

Pita bread, for serving

In a medium bowl, combine the bulgur with the hot water. Let stand until the bulgur is tender, about 25 minutes; drain any excess water.

Meanwhile, in a large bowl, combine the scallions, cucumbers, chickpeas, parsley, mint, lemon juice, oil, salt, and pepper. Add the bulgur and toss well. Serve with the pita bread.

COOK'S TIP: Soak and drain the bulgur 1 day in advance, cover, and refrigerate. Toss with the remaining ingredients for a last-minute salad in less than 10 minutes. Refrigerate in an airtight container for up to 4 days.

Quinoa-Walnut-Celery Salad

Prep time: 15 minutes
Total time: 35 minutes
Serves 4 to 6

This crunchy, nutty salad is a great dish to keep on hand for when hunger strikes. Quinoa (pronounced keen-*wah*) is a complete protein, containing all nine essential amino acids, so the salad has staying power. Because it is really a plant (though it resembles a grain), quinoa is wheat- and gluten-free, and it contains about twice as much calcium as many grains.

1 cup walnut halves

1 cup quinoa

4 ribs celery, thinly sliced

4 scallions (white and light green parts), thinly sliced

1 cup loosely packed fresh flat-leaf parsley, chopped

¼ cup extra-virgin olive oil

2 tablespoons freshly squeezed lemon juice (from about 1 lemon)

1 teaspoon kosher salt

¼ teaspoon freshly ground black pepper

Preheat the oven to 400°F.

Spread the walnuts on a baking sheet and bake until toasted and fragrant, 6 to 8 minutes. When cool enough to handle, coarsely chop.

In a small saucepan, combine the quinoa with 2 cups of water and bring to a boil. Decrease the heat, cover, and simmer until the quinoa is tender and the water is absorbed, 12 to 15 minutes. Spread the quinoa on a baking sheet and let cool.

Meanwhile, in a large bowl, combine the celery, walnuts, scallions, parsley, oil, lemon juice, salt, and pepper. Fold in the cooled quinoa.

Refrigerate in an airtight container for up to 4 days.

Six More Ways to Nourish a Friend on the Mend

When a person is ill, best-laid plans often go awry. So, bring dishes that can easily be reheated or frozen, in case the family can't eat your meal on the scheduled delivery night. Here are six more tips for easing the burden faced by a recuperating friend or relative and his or her family.

• Call or e-mail in advance to ask what day and time is best for your delivery. Most people have limited freezer and refrigerator space and can't handle four pans of lasagne at once.

• Organize a meal train. Serve as liaison between the patient's family and volunteer cooks, streamlining communication and setting a delivery schedule. For details, see How to Organize a Meal Train on page 19.

• Bring a complete meal. You'll save the caregiver a trip to the supermarket for greens to add to a lone casserole. If you're short on time, cook a main dish and stop at the store for a bagged salad kit and loaf of fresh, whole-grain bread. In some cases, bread may be the only food a patient finds appetizing, and fresh bread makes for yummy toast the next day.

• Avoid burdening a stressed household with Tupperware anxiety. Deliver the meal in food storage boxes or disposable pans that you don't need back, or schedule a pickup, asking your friend to simply leave roasting pans or glassware on his or her porch for you to retrieve.

• If you run out of time to cook, bring a restaurant gift card. A family that has been cooped up may be craving their favorite dishes from the local Thai restaurant or pizza joint.

• Bring a bottle of wine for the caregiver.

Turkey and Dill Meatloaf

Prep time: 15 minutes
Total time: 1 hour
Serves 4 to 6

Using turkey in place of beef reduces the saturated fat in this comforting classic. Packing the meatloaf with veggies boosts the nutritional value, and the dill adds a tasty twist. meatloaf always makes for great leftovers.

2 tablespoons olive oil

1 medium yellow onion, chopped

1½ pounds ground turkey

1 cup grated zucchini (about 1 medium)

1 cup loosely packed fresh flat-leaf parsley, chopped

½ cup loosely packed fresh dill, chopped

½ cup dry bread crumbs

½ cup (2 ounces) grated Parmesan cheese

3 tablespoons Dijon mustard

1 large egg

¾ teaspoon kosher salt

¼ teaspoon freshly ground black pepper

Preheat the oven to 375°F. Lightly oil a 9 by 13-inch baking dish.

Heat the oil in a medium skillet over medium-high heat. Add the onion and cook, stirring often, until softened, 5 to 6 minutes.

Meanwhile, in a large bowl, using your hands or a wooden spoon, combine the turkey, zucchini, parsley, dill, bread crumbs, Parmesan, mustard, egg, salt, pepper, and the cooked onion.

Transfer the mixture to the prepared baking dish and shape into a 5 by 9-inch loaf. Bake to an internal temperature of 155°F, 40 to 50 minutes. Let rest for 5 minutes before slicing.

COOK'S TIP: Before freezing a cooked meatloaf, let it cool completely. Wrap tightly with plastic wrap and then with aluminum foil, and freeze for up to 2 months. To thaw, transfer to the refrigerator overnight.

Roasted Cauliflower Macaroni and Cheese

Prep time: 40 minutes
Total time: 1 hour
Serves 6 to 8

With the addition of roasted cauliflower, this mac 'n' cheese is a more grown-up rendition of every family's favorite. Cauliflower adds extra texture, a hint of natural sweetness, and a boost of fiber and vitamin C. To round out the meal, deliver the casserole with one of the Butter Lettuce Salad variations on page 12.

1 medium head cauliflower, cut into small florets

3 tablespoons olive oil

1 teaspoon kosher salt

¼ teaspoon freshly ground black pepper

1 pound elbow macaroni

4 tablespoons (½ stick) unsalted butter

½ cup all-purpose flour, spooned and leveled

5½ cups whole milk

2 cups (8 ounces) grated extra-sharp cheddar cheese

½ cup (2 ounces) grated Parmesan cheese, plus ¼ cup for sprinkling

Pinch of freshly grated nutmeg

Preheat the oven to 375°F. Butter a 3-quart casserole dish.

On a rimmed baking sheet, toss together the cauliflower, oil, ½ teaspoon of the salt, and ⅛ teaspoon of the pepper. Roast, stirring once, until golden and tender, about 25 minutes.

Meanwhile, cook the pasta for 2 minutes less than the package cooking time; it should be less than al dente. Drain.

Melt the butter in a large saucepan over medium heat. Add the flour and cook, stirring, for 2 minutes. Add the milk, a little at a time at first, whisking until smooth after each addition. Bring to a boil, then decrease the heat and simmer, stirring often, until the sauce has thickened, 6 to 8 minutes. Remove from the heat and stir in the cheddar, Parmesan, nutmeg, and the remaining ½ teaspoon salt and ⅛ teaspoon pepper. Stir in the pasta and cauliflower.

Pour the mixture into the prepared casserole and sprinkle with more Parmesan. Bake until bubbling and golden brown on top, 20 to 25 minutes.

COOK'S TIP: For that go-to meal for one or two, freeze leftover macaroni and cheese in individual portions in resealable plastic bags. To bake directly from the freezer, remove from the bag, place in a baking dish, cover with aluminum foil, and bake at 375°F until heated through, 30 to 40 minutes. If you are watching your saturated fat intake, you can use 2 percent milk with this recipe, but don't use skim.

Chicken Cacciatore with Mashed Potatoes

Prep time: 35 minutes
Total time: 1 hour
Serves 4

This homey, satisfying staple just plain makes you want to get out of bed. The dish reheats well, so there is no pressure to deliver it piping hot.

2 tablespoons olive oil

1 (3½- to 4-pound) chicken, cut into 10 pieces (each breast halved)

1 teaspoon kosher salt

½ teaspoon freshly ground black pepper

1 pound button mushrooms, quartered

2 cloves garlic, chopped

1 (28-ounce) can diced tomatoes with juice

1 tablespoon coarsely chopped fresh rosemary

Mashed potatoes (recipe follows)

Preheat the oven to 400°F.

Heat 1 tablespoon of the oil in a large wide-bottomed saucepan or skillet over medium-high heat. Season the chicken with ½ teaspoon of the salt and ¼ teaspoon of the pepper and cook until browned, 6 to 8 minutes per side. Transfer the chicken to a large baking dish. Pour off any drippings left in the pan, but leave the brown bits.

Heat the remaining 1 tablespoon oil in the same saucepan over medium-high heat. Add the mushrooms and cook, scraping up the brown bits with a wooden spoon, until the mushrooms are tender and the juices have evaporated, 6 to 8 minutes. Stir in the garlic and cook for 1 minute. Add the tomatoes, rosemary, and the remaining ½ teaspoon salt and ¼ teaspoon pepper and bring to a boil. Pour the sauce over the chicken and roast until the chicken is cooked through, 20 to 25 minutes. Serve with the mashed potatoes.

Mashed Potatoes

Serves 4

2 pounds Yukon Gold or other waxy potatoes (about 4 medium), peeled and quartered

¾ cup whole milk

4 tablespoons (½ stick) unsalted butter

¾ teaspoon kosher salt

¼ teaspoon freshly ground black pepper

Place the potatoes in a medium saucepan, cover with cold water, and bring to a boil. Add a large pinch of salt, decrease the heat, and simmer until the potatoes are tender when pierced with a paring knife, 15 to 18 minutes. Drain the potatoes and mash with the milk, butter, salt, and pepper.

COOK'S TIP: If you wish to make this chicken dish a day in advance and store it in the refrigerator, reheating will take only 20 minutes in a 400°F oven. As for the mashed potatoes, reheat them in a bowl set over a pot of simmering water and stir occasionally until heated through, or the microwave will do the trick. Refrigerate both dishes in an airtight container for up to 4 days or freeze for up to 1 month.

Rosemary Beef with Roasted Tomatoes and Potatoes

Prep time: 15 minutes
Total time: 1 hour 30 minutes
Serves 4 to 6

When you are regaining your appetite, sometimes there is just no substitute for beef. This simply seasoned, one-pan meal is plenty for a family of four, with enough leftovers for an amazing roast beef and tomato sandwich. Either roast this dish at home or deliver it ready to roast, along with the simple cooking instructions.

1½ pounds baby red potatoes, quartered

1 pint grape tomatoes

¼ cup olive oil

1½ teaspoons kosher salt

¾ teaspoon freshly ground black pepper

3 pounds beef roast, such as rib, rump, or sirloin tip

4 cloves garlic, finely chopped

1 tablespoon chopped fresh rosemary

Preheat the oven to 350°F.

On a rimmed baking sheet, combine the potatoes, tomatoes, 3 tablespoons of the oil, ½ teaspoon of the salt, and ¼ teaspoon of the pepper.

Season the meat with the remaining 1 teaspoon salt and ½ teaspoon pepper and place in the middle of the pan, pushing the vegetables aside as necessary.

In a small bowl, combine the garlic, rosemary, and the remaining 1 tablespoon oil. Rub evenly over the meat. Roast the meat to the desired doneness, stirring the vegetables once, about 1 hour 15 minutes for medium-rare (130°F internal temperature). Let rest for 10 minutes before slicing.

Halibut, Leek, and Carrot Parchment Packets

Prep time: 15 minutes
Total time: 30 minutes
Serves 4

Cooking in parchment is a flavorful and healthful way to steam delicate fish and vegetables. Feel free to vary your ingredients, substituting scallops or flounder for the halibut and a mixture of thinly sliced bell peppers, fennel, and thyme for the leeks and carrots.

3 leeks (white and light green parts), halved lengthwise and sliced into thin half-moons

2 medium carrots, peeled and sliced into thin rounds

4 (6-ounce) pieces halibut fillet (1 inch thick)

¾ teaspoon kosher salt

¼ teaspoon freshly ground black pepper

¼ cup extra-virgin olive oil

2 tablespoons fresh oregano leaves

Preheat the oven to 400°F.

Cut four 12-inch squares of parchment paper and fold each crosswise in half. Open the parchment and, dividing evenly, place the leeks and carrots in the center of each sheet, along the crease. Top each vegetable pile with the fish and season with salt and pepper. Drizzle with the oil and sprinkle with the oregano. Fold the parchment over the fish, making small overlapping folds along the edges to seal.

Place on a baking sheet and bake for 12 minutes. Transfer the entire packets to plates, split with a knife to open, and enjoy.

COOK'S TIP: Deliver these packets, uncooked, with the simple cooking instructions so that they can be enjoyed straight from the oven at any given time. Cook within 2 days of delivery or freeze for up to 1 month in a resealable plastic bag. Thaw in the refrigerator before baking.

Stewed Chicken with Chickpeas and Lemon

Prep time: 25 minutes
Total time: 1 hour
Serves 4

This brothy chicken dish is soothing and light, leaving you feeling satisfied but not stuffed. The earthy flavors of cumin and cinnamon make it something to savor.

2 tablespoons olive oil

2 medium yellow onions, thinly sliced

5 medium carrots (about 1 pound), cut into 2-inch sticks

1½ teaspoons kosher salt

1½ teaspoons paprika

¾ teaspoon ground cumin

¼ teaspoon ground cinnamon

¼ teaspoon freshly ground black pepper

4 strips lemon zest (use a vegetable peeler)

1 (3½- to 4-pound) chicken, cut into 10 pieces (each breast halved)

1 (15.5-ounce) can chickpeas, rinsed and drained

1 cup loosely packed fresh flat-leaf parsley, chopped

1 cup couscous

Heat the oil in a large, wide-bottomed saucepan over medium-high heat. Add the onions, carrots, and ¾ teaspoon of the salt and cook, stirring often, until beginning to soften, 8 to 10 minutes (decrease the heat, as necessary, to prevent scorching). Add the paprika, cumin, cinnamon, pepper, and lemon zest and cook, stirring, for 1 minute.

Remove and discard the skin from the chicken. Nestle the chicken in the vegetables and add enough water to cover (about 2½ cups); bring to a boil. Decrease the heat and simmer, partially covered, until the chicken is cooked through, 35 to 40 minutes. Stir in the chickpeas, parsley, and the remaining ¾ teaspoon salt and simmer for a few minutes more to heat through.

Meanwhile, in a small saucepan, bring 1 cup of water with a pinch of salt to a boil.

Add the couscous, stir quickly, cover, and remove from the heat. Let stand for 5 minutes. Fluff with a fork before serving. Serve with the chicken.

COOK'S TIP: The stew and couscous can be made a day in advance; they reheat well. Deliver the stew in its pot for easy stovetop reheating, and bring the couscous in a resealable plastic bag for a quick turn in the microwave. Make arrangements for pot pickup.

Zucchini and Parmesan Frittata

Prep time: 15 minutes
Total time: 30 minutes
Serves 6 to 8

This zesty egg dish is one of the easiest in the book, requiring just six ingredients—and that includes the salt and pepper! Delicious either hot or cold, it's the perfect energy boost at any hour. For breakfast, serve the frittata with fruit; for lunch or dinner, serve with the Arugula, Radish, Cucumber, and Olive Salad on page 14. Or keep it in the fridge for a savory snack.

1 tablespoon olive oil

4 medium zucchini (about 1½ pounds), cut into thin rounds

¾ teaspoon kosher salt

¼ teaspoon freshly ground black pepper

8 large eggs, beaten

¼ cup (1 ounce) grated Parmesan cheese, plus more for sprinkling

Preheat the oven to 375°F.

Heat the oil in a medium ovenproof skillet over medium-high heat. Add the zucchini and cook, stirring often, until tender, about 10 minutes. Season with ¼ teaspoon of the salt and ⅛ teaspoon of the pepper.

Meanwhile, in a medium bowl, whisk together the eggs, Parmesan, and the remaining ½ teaspoon salt and ⅛ teaspoon pepper. Pour the egg mixture over the zucchini and sprinkle more Parmesan over the top. Transfer the skillet to the oven and bake until puffed and the center is just set, 15 to 18 minutes. Cut into wedges and serve warm or chilled.

Refrigerate, tightly wrapped, for up to 3 days.

Oat-Nut Scones

Prep time: 15 minutes
Total time: 30 minutes
Makes 16 scones

Warmed in the oven with a cup of hot tea and honey, this chewy, nutty scone will comfort any patient, day or night. It's also the perfect treat to keep on hand for visitors.

1 cup walnut halves

1½ cups all-purpose flour, spooned and leveled

½ cup granulated sugar

1½ teaspoons baking powder

¼ teaspoon baking soda

½ teaspoon kosher salt

¼ teaspoon ground cinnamon

Pinch of freshly grated nutmeg

½ cup (1 stick) cold unsalted butter, cut into small pieces

¾ cup buttermilk

1 cup old-fashioned rolled oats

Turbinado or raw sugar, for sprinkling

Preheat the oven to 400°F. Line 2 baking sheets with parchment paper.

Spread the walnuts on a baking sheet and bake until toasted and fragrant, 6 to 8 minutes. When cool enough to handle, coarsely chop.

In a large bowl, whisk together the flour, granulated sugar, baking powder, baking soda, salt, cinnamon, and nutmeg. Cut in the butter with a pastry blender or your fingers until coarse, irregular crumbs form. Stir in the buttermilk until just combined, then stir in the oats and walnuts.

Drop 2 heaping tablespoon–size mounds 2 inches apart onto the prepared baking sheets. Sprinkle with the turbinado sugar and bake until golden brown with crispy edges, 12 to 15 minutes. Let cool on a wire rack.

COOK'S TIP: If you use your fingers to blend in the butter, do so as quickly as possible so that the butter doesn't become too soft. Having those little butter pieces in the dough ensures a flaky and tender scone. Store in an airtight container for up to 2 days. Pop them in the oven for a few minutes to crisp the edges.

Zucchini-Orange Bread

Prep time: 15 minutes
Total time: 1 hour 30 minutes
Serves 8 to 10

Spiked with cinnamon and fragrant, fresh orange zest, this moist bread works for breakfast, a snack, or dessert. Select firm, bright green zucchini that are no longer than 8 inches, as larger ones can be bitter.

2 cups all-purpose flour, spooned and leveled

1 teaspoon ground cinnamon

1 teaspoon baking powder

¼ teaspoon baking soda

½ teaspoon kosher salt

2 large eggs

¾ cup sugar

½ cup canola oil

1 teaspoon pure vanilla extract

2 cups grated zucchini (about 2 medium)

1 teaspoon grated orange zest

Preheat the oven to 350°F. Lightly oil and flour an 8½ by 4½-inch loaf pan, tapping out the excess flour.

In a medium bowl, whisk together the flour, cinnamon, baking powder, baking soda, and salt.

In a large bowl, whisk together the eggs, sugar, oil, and vanilla. Stir in the zucchini and orange zest. Gradually stir in the flour mixture until just combined (do not overmix).

Scrape the batter evenly into the prepared pan and bake until a toothpick inserted into the center comes out with a few moist crumbs attached, 45 to 55 minutes. Let cool for 20 minutes in the pan on a wire rack before unmolding.

COOK'S TIP: This bread will keep, tightly wrapped, for up to 4 days. Freeze for up to 1 month wrapped tightly with plastic wrap, then with aluminum foil. Thaw in the refrigerator overnight.

Peanut Crunch Cookies

Prep time: 20 minutes
Total time: 50 minutes
Makes 48 cookies

Are you a crisp-cookie fan or more of a chewy-cookie lover? Either way, this cookie is for you. Loaded with peanut butter goodness, it has crisp edges and a slightly chewy center. Try using natural peanut butter for that intense, true peanut flavor. Just make sure it is well stirred.

2 cups all-purpose flour, spooned and leveled

1 teaspoon baking soda

¼ teaspoon baking powder

¼ teaspoon kosher salt

¾ cup (1½ sticks) unsalted butter, at room temperature

1 cup crunchy peanut butter

1 cup granulated sugar

¾ cup dark brown sugar

1 large egg

Preheat the oven to 350°F. Line 2 baking sheets with parchment paper.

In a medium bowl, whisk together the flour, baking soda, baking powder, and salt.

Working with a stand mixer, preferably fitted with the paddle attachment, or with a hand mixer with a large bowl, beat the butter, peanut butter, ¾ cup of the granulated sugar, and the brown sugar on medium speed until creamy. Beat in the egg. With the mixer on low speed, gradually mix in the flour mixture.

Shape the dough into tablespoon-size balls, then roll them in the remaining ¼ cup sugar.

Place them 2 inches apart on the prepared baking sheets. Using the tines of a fork, press a crosshatch pattern onto each cookie. Bake, rotating the sheets halfway through the baking time, until the edges are just set and the centers are still soft, 12 to 15 minutes (bake for the full 15 minutes if you like a crisper cookie). Let cool for 5 minutes on the baking sheets before transferring the cookies to wire racks.

CHAPTER 3

WELCOME TO THE NEIGHBORHOOD

Main Dishes and Gifts-in-a-Jar

- Jar of Quick Garlic-Dill Pickles
- Red and White Chili
- Cheddar-Scallion Cornbread
- Spaghetti Kit: Toasted Garlic Marinara, Pasta, and Fresh Bread
- Barbecue Spiced Chicken with Southwestern Slaw
- Savory Chicken Cobbler
- Roast Beef and Cheddar Sandwiches for the Movers

Sweet Treats

- Love Thy Neighbor Apple Pie
- Raspberry-Rhubarb Crumble Pie
- Extra-Fudgy Brownies
- Lemon-Glazed Pistachio Shortbread Cookies
- Apricot Crumble Bars
- Roasted Almond–Chocolate Chip Cookies

In these hectic times, it's an extraordinary gesture to knock on a new neighbor's door and introduce yourself with a plate of cookies. Show up with Raspberry-Rhubarb Crumble Pie (page 72) or Barbecue Spiced Chicken with Southwestern Slaw (page 66) and you may have new best friends for life. At the very least, you'll have an eager volunteer to water your ficus the next time you're on vacation.

Nothing works up an appetite like hauling boxes and maneuvering an armoire through the front door, so the recipes in this chapter have been created to really hit the spot. We've included satisfying treats that can be devoured immediately, like Apricot Crumble Bars (page 79) and Extra-Fudgy Brownies (page 74), plus filling main dishes that can be refrigerated or frozen. Your neighbors will be thrilled to pull Red and White Chili (page 63) from the fridge the day after they've unpacked, when they're too wiped out to cook and still can't find the box labeled "Pots and Pans."

This chapter also features tasty gifts-in-a-jar, like Toasted Garlic Marinara (page 65) and a Jar of Quick Garlic-Dill Pickles (page 62). You can make them in advance—perhaps when the "Sold" sign goes up next door—and have the jars ready when the moving truck pulls up on your street. If you're inspired to go a few extra miles, try our Roast Beef and Cheddar Sandwiches for the Movers (page 69). You'll save your neighbors a trip to the store to feed the hungry, sweaty guys who just moved the three-piece sectional down to the basement.

Jar of Quick Garlic-Dill Pickles

Prep time: 5 minutes
Total time: 4 hours
Makes 1 quart

Crisp, crunchy, and aromatic, these pickles are unbelievably easy to make. (But who needs to know that?)

4 Kirby cucumbers (about 1 pound), quartered lengthwise into spears

¾ cup white vinegar

1 tablespoon sugar

2 teaspoons kosher salt

1 teaspoon dill seeds

1 teaspoon black peppercorns

½ teaspoon crushed red pepper (optional)

2 cloves garlic, smashed

Place the cucumber spears in a 1-quart jar with a tight-fitting lid.

In a medium bowl, combine the vinegar, sugar, salt, dill seeds, peppercorns, crushed red pepper, and garlic with ¾ cup of very hot tap water, stirring until the sugar is dissolved. Pour into the jar of cucumbers and seal with the lid. Refrigerate for at least 6 hours before eating and for up to 2 weeks.

COOK'S TIP: Using the ratio of vinegar, water, and salt in this recipe, you can get creative and make pickles with additional seasoning ingredients, such as thinly sliced onion, mustard seeds, coriander seeds, cumin seeds, celery seeds, and fresh dill. Or you can increase the amount of sugar for a sweeter pickle.

Red and White Chili

Prep time: 20 minutes
Total time: 45 minutes
Serve 6 to 8

After a hard day of hauling boxes, nothing refuels the tank like a big bowl of chili. Loaded with beans and ground beef and laced with cinnamon, this chili is mild enough for the entire family, but for more of a kick, stir in cayenne pepper. If you're feeling especially neighborly, bring Cheddar-Scallion Cornbread (page 64), too. For neighbors who have not yet unpacked, deliver the chili in a pot for reheating, along with a serving spoon, bowls, and spoons. Arrange for a next-day pot pickup—you won't have to travel far.

2 tablespoons olive oil

1 large yellow onion, chopped

2 medium green bell peppers, cut into ½-inch pieces

2 cloves garlic, finely chopped

1½ teaspoons kosher salt

2 tablespoons chili powder

1½ teaspoons ground cumin

Pinch of ground cinnamon

¼ cup tomato paste

1½ pounds ground chuck beef

1 (14.5-ounce) can diced tomatoes with juice

2 (15.5-ounce) cans cannellini beans, rinsed and drained

2 (15.5-ounce) cans kidney beans, rinsed and drained

1 tablespoon dark brown sugar

¼ teaspoon freshly ground black pepper

Heat the oil in a large pot over medium-high heat. Add the onion, bell peppers, garlic, and ½ teaspoon of the salt and cook, stirring often, until tender, 8 to 10 minutes (decrease the heat, as necessary, to prevent scorching).

Stir in the chili powder, cumin, and cinnamon, then the tomato paste, and cook, stirring, for 2 minutes. Add the beef and cook, crumbling with a spoon, until no longer pink, 6 to 8 minutes. Stir in the tomatoes, 3 cups water, the cannellini and kidney beans, sugar, pepper, and the remaining 1 teaspoon salt and bring to a boil.

Decrease the heat and simmer until thickened, about 20 minutes.

COOK'S TIP: Ground turkey can easily be substituted for the beef. Refrigerate in an airtight container for up to 4 days or freeze for up to 2 months.

Cheddar-Scallion Cornbread

Prep time: 10 minutes
Total time: 40 minutes
Serves 8

The sharp, nutty taste of cheddar, combined with scallion, creates a savory cornbread, not your typical sweet variety. It's a perfect accompaniment to the Red and White Chili (page 63) or the Barbecue Spiced Chicken with Southwestern Slaw (page 66).

1 cup all-purpose flour, spooned and leveled

1 cup cornmeal

2 tablespoons sugar

2 teaspoons baking powder

½ teaspoon baking soda

¾ teaspoon kosher salt

⅛ teaspoon freshly ground black pepper

1 cup buttermilk

6 tablespoons (¾ stick) unsalted butter, melted

1 large egg, beaten

1 cup (4 ounces) grated sharp cheddar cheese

2 scallions (white and light green parts), chopped

Preheat the oven to 350°F. Butter or spray with nonstick cooking spray a 9-inch round cake pan and line the bottom with parchment paper.

In a large bowl, whisk together the flour, cornmeal, sugar, baking powder, baking soda, salt, and pepper and make a well in the center.

Add the buttermilk, butter, and egg and stir until just combined (do not overmix). Stir in the cheddar and scallions.

Scrape the batter into the prepared pan and bake until a toothpick inserted into the center comes out clean, 26 to 30 minutes. Let cool for 20 minutes in the pan. Invert the bread onto a plate, remove the parchment, and invert again to serve it top side up.

Spaghetti Kit: Toasted Garlic Marinara, Pasta, and Fresh Bread

Deliver a jar of this garlicky marinara with a 1-pound box of spaghetti or penne and a loaf of fresh bread. The sauce is a cinch to make, and your neighbors will be mighty impressed that it's homemade. If you have the time to make it, the Caesar-Like Salad with Croutons (page 15) rounds out the meal perfectly.

Toasted Garlic Marinara

Prep time: 10 minutes
Total time: 25 minutes
Makes about 4 cups

2 tablespoons olive oil

8 cloves garlic, sliced

2 (28-ounce cans) whole peeled tomatoes with juice

1 teaspoon dried oregano

1 teaspoon sugar

¾ teaspoon kosher salt

½ teaspoon crushed red pepper

¼ teaspoon freshly ground black pepper

Heat the oil in a large saucepan over medium-high heat. Add the garlic and cook, stirring, until light golden brown, 1 to 2 minutes. Add the tomatoes, oregano, sugar, salt, red pepper, and black pepper and bring to a boil. Decrease the heat and simmer, breaking up the tomatoes with a spoon, until slightly thickened, about 20 minutes.

COOK'S TIP: Fresh garlic is always best. Jarred garlic, while convenient, is often overly pungent, with a funky aftertaste. Refrigerate the sauce in an airtight container for up to 5 days or freeze for up to 2 months.

Barbecue Spiced Chicken with Southwestern Slaw

Prep time: 20 minutes
Total time: 55 minutes
Serves 4

Quick to prepare, this chicken-with-a-kick is great hot or at room temperature—it's even better cold. And what's barbecued chicken without coleslaw? You can make the mayo-free slaw while the chicken is roasting.

1 (3½- to 4-pound) chicken, cut into 10 pieces (each breast halved)

1 tablespoon olive oil

1 tablespoon sweet paprika

2 teaspoons dark brown sugar

1 teaspoon ground cumin

1 teaspoon kosher salt

½ teaspoon freshly ground black pepper

½ teaspoon cayenne pepper

Southwestern Slaw (recipe follows)

Preheat the oven to 425°F. Place the chicken in a large roasting pan and drizzle with the oil.

In a small bowl, combine the paprika, sugar, cumin, salt, black pepper, and cayenne pepper and rub over the chicken. Roast until cooked through, 35 to 40 minutes.

Serve hot, at room temperature, or cold, with the slaw.

Southwestern Slaw

Prep time: 15 minutes
Total time: 15 minutes
Serves 6 to 8

1 cup sour cream

¼ cup freshly squeezed lime juice (from about 2 limes)

¾ teaspoon kosher salt

¼ teaspoon freshly ground black pepper

1 small green cabbage (2 pounds), quartered, cored, and thinly sliced (about 8 cups)

2 medium carrots, grated (1 cup)

1 cup loosely packed fresh cilantro, chopped

4 scallions (white and light green parts), thinly sliced

2 jalapeño chiles, quartered lengthwise, seeded, and sliced

¾ cup golden raisins

In a large bowl, whisk together the sour cream, lime juice, salt, and pepper. Add the cabbage, carrots, cilantro, scallions, jalapeños, and raisins and toss to combine.

Refrigerate in an airtight container for up to 3 days.

Savory Chicken Cobbler

Prep time: 25 minutes
Total time: 1 hour 15 minutes
Serves 8

This is a rendition of chicken and dumplings with the savory biscuits baked atop, rather than steamed in, a creamy corn, red pepper, and chicken filling. The result: a flaky and tender topping that is something to savor. Deliver the cobbler fresh out of the oven or deliver it ready-to-bake with the simple baking instructions.

10 tablespoons (1¼ sticks) cold unsalted butter, cut into pieces

1 medium onion, chopped

1 red bell pepper, cored and cut into ½-inch pieces

1 teaspoon kosher salt

3 cups corn (from 3 large ears, or 1 pound frozen)

2 cups heavy cream

1 cup low-sodium chicken broth

1 (2- to 2½-pound) rotisserie chicken

¼ teaspoon freshly ground black pepper

2 cups all-purpose flour, spooned and leveled

2 teaspoons baking powder

1 cup whole or 2% milk

1 tablespoon fresh thyme leaves

Preheat the oven to 375°F.

Melt 2 tablespoons of the butter in a large saucepan over medium-high heat. Add the onion, bell pepper, and ½ teaspoon of the salt and cook, stirring often, until softened, 6 to 7 minutes. Stir in the corn, cream, and chicken broth and bring to a boil. Remove the meat from the chicken, shred, and stir into the corn mixture, then pour into a 9 by 13-inch baking dish.

Meanwhile, in a medium bowl, whisk together the flour, baking powder, and the remaining ½ teaspoon salt. With a pastry blender or your fingers, cut in the remaining 8 tablespoons butter until coarse, irregular crumbs form. Stir in the milk and thyme until just combined (it will be a very moist dough). Scoop 12 heaping spoonfuls over the chicken mixture and bake until the tops are golden brown, about 45 minutes.

Roast Beef and Cheddar Sandwiches for the Movers

Prep time: 10 minutes
Total time: 10 minutes
Serves 4

Loaded with roast beef, cheddar, and a little horseradish, these sandwiches are hefty enough to satisfy movers who have just unloaded the contents of a four-bedroom house!

3 tablespoons mayonnaise

1 tablespoon prepared horseradish

8 slices sourdough bread

8 ounces thinly sliced roast beef

4 ounces sliced cheddar cheese

4 leaves butter lettuce

2 medium beefsteak tomatoes, sliced

Pinch of kosher salt and freshly ground black pepper

In a small bowl, combine the mayonnaise and horseradish and spread over each slice of bread. On 4 of the slices, layer the roast beef, cheddar, lettuce, and tomatoes. Season with the salt and pepper and top with the remaining 4 slices of bread.

Love Thy Neighbor Apple Pie

Prep time: 1 hour
Total time: 4 hours (includes cooling time)
Serves 8

Nothing is more iconic than delivering a pie to a new neighbor. This old-fashioned favorite is brightened up with lemon and a hint of honey. For an extra touch, use a combination of the suggested apples.

Crust

2½ cups all-purpose flour, spooned and leveled

2 teaspoons sugar, plus more for sprinkling

½ teaspoon kosher salt

1 cup (2 sticks) cold unsalted butter, cut into small pieces

2 teaspoons cider vinegar

6 to 8 tablespoons ice-cold water

Filling

2½ pounds apples (Granny Smith, Winesap, or Golden Delicious), peeled and thinly sliced

2 tablespoons all-purpose flour, spooned and leveled

1 tablespoon freshly squeezed lemon juice

2 tablespoons honey

¼ teaspoon ground cinnamon

⅔ cup sugar

For the crust, in the bowl of a food processor, pulse the flour, the sugar, and the salt. Add the butter and pulse until large, pea-size clumps form. Add the vinegar and 6 tablespoons of the water. Pulse a few times, until the dough holds together when squeezed (if necessary, add 1 or 2 more tablespoons of water and pulse twice more). Turn the dough (it will be crumbly) out onto a work surface and gather together. Divide in half, shape into disks, wrap with plastic wrap, and refrigerate for at least 20 minutes.

Preheat the oven to 400°F with the rack in the lowest position.

On a floured work surface, roll the bottom crust to ⅛ inch thick and 12 inches in diameter. Transfer to a 9-inch pie plate and refrigerate.

Meanwhile, for the filling, in a large bowl, toss together the apples, flour, lemon juice, honey, cinnamon, and sugar. Transfer the apple mixture to the pie shell.

Roll out the top crust to ⅛ inch thick and 12 inches in diameter, and lay over the fruit. Tuck the overhang under the bottom crust, pressing slightly to help seal. Crimp the edges. Brush the top with water or a beaten egg and sprinkle with sugar. Using the tip of a paring knife, cut vents into the top crust.

Place the pie on a baking sheet and bake, rotating halfway through the baking time, until the crust is a deep golden brown and the fruit is bubbling, 55 to 60 minutes. Transfer to a wire rack to cool for at least 2 hours before slicing.

COOK'S TIP: Undoubtedly, pies are a labor of love. To break up the prep time, keep disks of tightly wrapped dough on hand in the freezer. Thaw in the refrigerator overnight.

Raspberry-Rhubarb Crumble Pie

Prep time: 45 minutes
Total time: 4 hours (includes cooling time)
Serves 8

Rhubarb is sour and unbearably tart and, strangely enough, the perfect partner to raspberries and ginger. When shopping for rhubarb, look for stalks that are deep red in color and that are perky, not limp.

Crust

1¼ cups all-purpose flour, spooned and leveled

2 teaspoons sugar

½ teaspoon kosher salt

½ cup (1 stick) cold unsalted butter, cut into small pieces

3 to 4 tablespoons ice-cold water

Crumble Topping

¾ cup all-purpose flour, spooned and leveled

¼ cup sugar

2 teaspoons grated fresh ginger

½ cup (1 stick) cold unsalted butter, cut into small pieces

Filling

1 pound rhubarb, cut into ½-inch pieces

12 ounces fresh raspberries

1 cup sugar

3 tablespoons all-purpose flour, leveled

Preheat the oven to 400°F with the rack in the lowest position.

For the crust, in the bowl of a food processor, pulse the flour, sugar, and salt. Add the butter and pulse until large, pea-size clumps form. Add 3 tablespoons of the water. Pulse a few times, until the dough holds together when squeezed (if necessary, add 1 more tablespoon of water and pulse twice more). Turn the dough (it will be crumbly) out onto a work surface and gather together. Shape into a disk, wrap with plastic wrap, and refrigerate for at least 20 minutes.

For the crumble topping, in the bowl of the food processor (no need to wash), pulse the flour, sugar, and ginger. Add the butter and pulse until crumbly and it holds together when squeezed. Transfer to a bowl and refrigerate until ready to use.

For the filling, in a large bowl, toss together the rhubarb, raspberries, sugar, and flour.

On a floured work surface, roll the dough to ⅛ inch thick and 12 inches in diameter. Transfer to a 9-inch pie plate, fold the edges under, and crimp. Fill the shell with the fruit filling and sprinkle with the crumble topping. Place the pie on a baking sheet and bake until the top is golden and the fruit is bubbling, 55 to 60 minutes. Transfer to a wire rack to cool for at least 2 hours before slicing.

COOK'S TIP: For a flaky, delicate crust, work the dough as little as possible; do not overmix or overknead.

Extra-Fudgy Brownies

Prep time: 20 minutes
Total time: 2 hours (includes cooling time)
Makes 32 brownies

With just a few more ingredients than a box mix, these brownies are as easy to make and twice as good. To add your own signature, mix in chopped pecans or walnuts, chopped miniature peanut butter cups, chocolate chips, chopped peppermint patties, or a spoonful of instant espresso powder.

1 cup (2 sticks) unsalted butter

12 ounces bittersweet chocolate, finely chopped

5 large eggs

2 cups granulated sugar

½ cup dark brown sugar

1 teaspoon pure vanilla extract

¾ teaspoon kosher salt

1 cup all-purpose flour, spooned and leveled

Preheat the oven to 350°F. Butter a 9 by 13-inch baking pan.

Melt the butter in a medium saucepan over medium heat. Remove from the heat and stir in the chocolate until melted and smooth. Let cool, but it should remain pourable.

Working with a stand mixer fitted with the whisk attachment, or with a hand mixer with a large bowl, beat the eggs, granulated sugar, brown sugar, vanilla, and salt on medium-high speed until pale and fluffy, 4 to 5 minutes. Using a rubber spatula, gently fold in the chocolate mixture (a few streaks remaining are okay).

‖‖

COOK'S TIP: Bittersweet chocolate has a high percentage of chocolate liquor with little added sugar, resulting in a rich, oh-so-fudgy brownie. High-quality chocolate contains fewer additives, further enhancing the chocolate flavor. Store your chocolate tightly wrapped in a cool, dry, dark place (avoid the refrigerator, as chocolate can easily pick up other odors). Store the brownies, tightly wrapped, for up to 4 days.

Fold in the flour until just combined (do not overmix).

Scrape the batter into the prepared pan and bake
until a toothpick inserted into the center comes out
with a few moist crumbs attached and a shiny crust
has formed, 25 to 30 minutes. Let cool for at least
1 hour on a wire rack before slicing.

Lemon-Glazed Pistachio Shortbread Cookies

Prep time: 25 minutes
Total time: 1 hour 45 minutes
Makes 40 cookies

The fresh lemon juice and lemon zest give these crisp and buttery shortbreads a zesty kick.

1½ cups all-purpose flour, spooned and leveled

½ cup cornstarch

¼ teaspoon kosher salt

14 tablespoons (1¾ sticks) unsalted butter, at room temperature

2½ cups confectioners' sugar

¼ cup shelled pistachios, finely chopped

1 teaspoon grated lemon zest (from 1 lemon)

3 tablespoons freshly squeezed lemon juice (from 1 lemon)

Preheat the oven to 350°F. Line 2 baking sheets with parchment paper.

In a medium bowl, whisk together the flour, cornstarch, and salt.

Working with a stand mixer, preferably fitted with the paddle attachment, or with a hand mixer with a large bowl, beat the butter and 1 cup of the confectioners' sugar on medium speed until smooth. With the mixer on low speed, gradually mix in the flour mixture until just combined and it holds together when squeezed (it will be slightly crumbly). Stir in the pistachios.

Gather the dough into a disk. On a lightly floured surface, roll the dough out to a generous ¼ inch thick. Cut into rounds with a 1½-inch cookie cutter and place 2 inches apart onto the prepared baking sheets, rerolling and cutting the scraps as necessary. Refrigerate until firm, about 30 minutes.

COOK'S TIP: You can easily alter the flavor of the glaze by substituting other citrus, such as orange, lime, or grapefruit. Store the cookies in an airtight container for up to 5 days.

Bake until the edges are set and light golden brown, 12 to 15 minutes. Transfer to a wire rack and let cool completely.

Meanwhile, in a medium bowl, whisk together the remaining 1½ cups confectioners' sugar, lemon zest, and lemon juice until smooth. Place the wire rack over a baking sheet to catch any drips. Dip the tops of the cookies into the glaze and place on the rack. Let set for 15 minutes.

Offering an
Extra Welcome

To make your new neighbors feel especially welcome, package your apple pie or spaghetti kit with a list of best local picks, like the optometrist you adore or the hole-in-the-wall coffeehouse that makes the planet's best lavender latte. Consider including your favorite:

- Restaurants, including pizza, Chinese, Thai, Mexican, Italian, bakery, coffee shop, and wine shop

- Grocery store or supermarket

- Farmer's market

- Dry cleaners

- Park and dog park

- Jogging and cycling routes

- Hardware store

- Movie theaters

- Medical professionals

- Driving shortcuts and parking tips

Apricot Crumble Bars

Prep time: 15 minutes
Total time: 1 hour 40 minutes (includes cooling time)
Makes 32 squares

The oats and pecans in this shortbread-like bar cookie provide a chewy, crunchy contrast to the sweet, gooey apricot preserves. You'll make these again and again!

1½ cups all-purpose flour, spooned and leveled

¾ cup sugar

½ teaspoon kosher salt

1 cup (2 sticks) cold unsalted butter, cut into pieces

1 cup pecans, chopped

1 cup old-fashioned rolled oats

¾ cup apricot preserves

Preheat the oven to 375°F. Butter a 9 by 13-inch baking pan.

In the bowl of a food processor, pulse the flour, sugar, and salt. Add the butter and pulse several times, until the dough comes together. Transfer to a large bowl and gently knead in the pecans and oats.

Reserve ½ cup of the dough and press the remaining dough into the prepared pan. Spread the preserves in a thin, even layer over the dough, leaving a ¼-inch border around the edges. Crumble the remaining dough over the preserves.

Bake until the edges are golden, 25 to 30 minutes. Let cool for at least 1 hour on a wire rack before slicing.

COOK'S TIP: Resist the temptation to add extra apricot preserves; otherwise, the bars won't hold their shape when sliced. Store in an airtight container for up to 4 days.

Roasted Almond–Chocolate Chip Cookies

Prep time: 20 minutes
Total time: 50 minutes
Makes 40 cookies

It has taken many pounds of butter and hundreds, maybe thousands, of pounds of chocolate chips to perfect this cookie. It's crispy on the outside, chewy on the inside, and sure to vanish quickly wherever it is served.

2 cups all-purpose flour, spooned and leveled

¾ teaspoon baking soda

¾ teaspoon kosher salt

12 tablespoons (1½ sticks) unsalted butter, at room temperature

1 cup firmly packed light brown sugar

¾ cup granulated sugar

1 large egg

2 teaspoons pure vanilla extract

2 cups (12 ounces) semisweet chocolate, chopped or chips

½ cup unsalted roasted almonds, chopped

Preheat the oven to 350°F. Line 2 baking sheets with parchment paper.

In a medium bowl, whisk together the flour, baking soda, and salt.

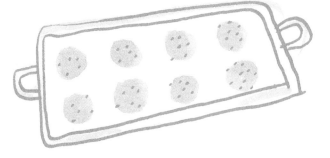

Working with a stand mixer, preferably fitted with the paddle attachment, or with a hand mixer with a large bowl, beat the butter, brown sugar, and granulated sugar on medium speed until creamy, 2 to 3 minutes. Beat in the egg and vanilla. With the mixer on low speed, gradually add the flour mixture. Stir in the chocolate chips and almonds.

Drop the dough in heaping tablespoon–size balls 2 inches apart onto the prepared baking sheets. Bake, rotating the sheets halfway through the baking time, until the edges are golden and the centers are just set, 12 to 15 minutes. Let the cookies cool for 5 minutes on the baking sheets before transferring them to a wire rack.

||||||||||||||||||||||||||||||||||||||||||||||||||||||||||||||||||||||||||||||||||||||||||||

COOK'S TIP: For a hot cookie every time, refrigerate the dough in a resealable plastic bag for up to 3 days, then follow the baking directions above. Or, drop the dough in heaping tablespoon–size balls on a baking sheet and freeze for 10 minutes, then transfer the balls to a resealable plastic bag and freeze for up to 1 month. When you are ready to bake, place the frozen cookies a good 2 inches apart on a parchment paper–lined baking sheet and bake for 18 to 20 minutes, until the edges are golden and the centers are just set.

CHAPTER 4

BLOCK PARTIES AND BARBECUES

Appetizers and Dips
- Chipotle-Pineapple Guacamole
- Sesame Crisps with Hummus
- Cucumber, Feta, and Dill Salsa
- Roasted Red Pepper Dip

Salads
- Cucumber and Potato Salad with Mustard-Dill Vinaigrette
- Grilled Zucchini and Eggplant Salad with Basil
- Summer Corn Salad with Chiles, Lime, and Feta
- Prosciutto and Melon with Mozzarella and Mint
- Platter of Tomatoes with Pepperoncini Vinaigrette
- Thai Watermelon and Shrimp Salad
- Romaine Salad with Salami, Mozzarella, and Peppadew Peppers
- Grilled Corn on the Cob with Chipotle and Parsley Butters

Main Dishes
- Pepper Jack Chicken Enchiladas with Tomatillo Sauce
- Spiced Coffee–Rubbed Baby Back Ribs
- Soy-Ginger Chicken Drumsticks
- Lemon-Thyme Chicken Skewers

Sweet Treats
- Chocolate-Pecan Sheet Cake
- Right-Side-Up Peach Cake
- Blueberry-Blackberry Cobbler
- Peanut Butter Chip Chocolate Cookies

Organizing a block party is no small feat these days, considering how few of us know our neighbors. But a summer gathering on a cul-de-sac, with kids playing street hockey or hopscotch on the sidewalk, is always a delight. You leave thinking, Let's get together more often!

Often, that notion has an addendum: Next time, let's plan a better menu.

We suspect there's nothing in your neighborhood association's bylaws mandating that hot dogs, fried chicken, and Popsicles be served at the annual get-together. So why not start a new tradition—with Soy-Ginger Chicken Drumsticks (page 103), Thai Watermelon and Shrimp Salad (page 96), and Right-Side-Up Peach Cake (page 106). The recipes in this chapter promise to take your block party or backyard barbecue up several notches.

If you're stepping up to bring a main dish to the party, or if you're hosting a summer gathering at your own house, you'll find several easy crowd-pleasers, such as Spiced Coffee–Rubbed Baby Back Ribs (page 102) and Pepper Jack Chicken Enchiladas with Tomatillo Sauce (page 100).

Alternatively, a great way to encourage mingling at summer get-togethers is to have guests bring their own meats or vegetarian "meats" to grill and to parcel out appetizers, side dishes, and desserts according to last name (A through H, appetizers; I through O, sides; P through Z, desserts). You'll find several knockouts here in each category. All of the dishes travel well, can be prepped and cooked before the event (or cooked and/or reheated on site), and are easy to double or triple to meet the needs of the crowd.

Recipes include tangy vegetable side dishes such as Summer Corn Salad with Chiles, Lime, and Feta (page 93) and fruit salad surprises such as Prosciutto and Melon with Mozzarella and Mint (page 94). Appetizers like tortilla chips with Chipotle-Pineapple Guacamole (page 86) are easy to eat while you swap gardening tips with the couple who just moved in down the street.

Chipotle-Pineapple Guacamole

Prep time: 15 minutes
Total time: 15 minutes
Serves 6 to 8

This guacamole takes a Mexican favorite to a new level with the addition of the smoky, spicy chipotle chiles in adobo sauce (smoked and canned jalapeños in red sauce) and the sweet, tropical flavors of pineapple. To dial down the heat without sacrificing flavor, use the adobo sauce without the chipotle pepper.

6 ripe avocados, halved and pitted

½ small red onion, chopped

¼ small pineapple, cut into ¼-inch pieces (about ½ cup)

1 cup loosely packed fresh cilantro, coarsely chopped

1 tablespoon freshly squeezed lime juice

1 tablespoon chopped chipotles in adobo sauce

¾ teaspoon kosher salt

Tortilla chips, for serving

Scoop out the meat of the avocados into a large bowl and gently mash. Stir in the onion, pineapple, cilantro, lime juice, chipotle, and salt. Serve with the tortilla chips.

COOK'S TIP: When choosing avocados, reach for the Hass avocado from California, with its dark, pebbly skin and creamy texture that is just ripe but a little firm. Make the guacamole up to 6 hours in advance, press plastic wrap directly on the guacamole to seal and prevent browning, and refrigerate until ready to serve.

Sesame Crisps with Hummus

Prep time: 15 minutes
Total time: 25 minutes
Serves 6 to 8

You'll never again pick up hummus at the store after you find out how easy and economical it is to make it yourself. This hummus gets its verve from lots of fresh lemon juice. The crisps are sprinkled with sumac, a deep red Middle Eastern spice with a lemony flavor; they are so addictive that you may need to make a double batch.

Crisps

6 pita breads, each split into 2 rounds
½ cup olive oil
¼ cup sesame seeds
¼ cup dried thyme
¾ teaspoon kosher salt
½ teaspoon sumac or paprika

Hummus

1 (15.5-ounce) can chickpeas, rinsed and drained
¼ cup olive oil
2 tablespoons freshly squeezed lemon juice
1 clove garlic
1 teaspoon ground cumin
½ teaspoon kosher salt

For the crisps, preheat the oven to 375°F.

Arrange the pita halves, cut side up, on a cutting board. In a small bowl, combine the oil, sesame seeds, thyme, salt, and sumac. Brush a thin layer over each pita and cut into triangles. Transfer to a baking sheet and bake until golden brown and crisp around the edges, about 10 minutes.

For the hummus, in a food processor, puree the chickpeas, oil, lemon juice, garlic, cumin, and salt until smooth. If necessary, add 1 to 2 tablespoons of warm water for your desired consistency. Serve with the sesame crisps.

COOK'S TIP: Refrigerate the hummus in an airtight container for up to 3 days. The sesame crisps are best served the same day they are made.

Cucumber, Feta, and Dill Salsa

Prep time: 10 minutes
Total time: 10 minutes
Serves 6 to 8

This crisp, fresh salsa is a snap to make and is so versatile that you'll find yourself spooning it onto turkey sandwiches or doubling the batch and tossing it with cooked and cooled short-shape pasta for a pasta salad.

3 Kirby cucumbers or 1 hothouse cucumber, cut into ¼-inch pieces

½ small red onion, finely chopped

½ cup loosely packed fresh dill, chopped

¼ cup extra-virgin olive oil

2 tablespoons freshly squeezed lemon juice

½ teaspoon kosher salt

¼ teaspoon freshly ground black pepper

1 cup (4 ounces) crumbled feta cheese

Crackers, for serving

In a medium bowl, combine the cucumbers, onion, dill, oil, lemon juice, salt, and pepper. Gently fold in the feta. Serve with the crackers.

COOK'S TIP: When choosing cucumbers, look for Kirby, Persian, or hothouse. They have a delicate skin that doesn't have to be peeled and smaller seeds than waxed cucumbers. If using waxed cucumbers, be sure to peel them.

Roasted Red Pepper Dip

Prep time: 10 minutes
Total time: 10 minutes
Serves 6 to 8

This dip uses three ingredients (roasted peppers, almonds, and Parmesan) that are delicious nibbles on their own; puree them together and you have a uniquely flavorful dip. Enjoy with breadsticks or any crunchy vegetable, such as carrots, radishes, cucumbers, or fennel.

1 (16-ounce) jar roasted red peppers, rinsed

½ cup unsalted roasted almonds

½ cup (2 ounces) grated Parmesan cheese

1 clove garlic

2 tablespoons olive oil

1 tablespoon sherry or red wine vinegar

¾ teaspoon kosher salt

Pinch of cayenne pepper

Breadsticks or cut-up vegetables, for serving

In the bowl of a food processor, puree the peppers, almonds, Parmesan, garlic, oil, vinegar, salt, and cayenne until smooth. Serve with the breadsticks or vegetables.

COOK'S TIP: Almonds are sold in the grocery store already roasted. Buy them unsalted, if you can, so that you have control of the salt content in the dip. Otherwise, add the salt a little at a time so you don't oversalt. Refrigerate the dip in an airtight container for up to 5 days.

What's in Season?
Nowadays you can buy cantaloupe in the dead of winter and pears in the heat of August, but those are likely flown in from another hemisphere or force-grown in artificial conditions, sacrificing freshness or flavor.

The fruits and vegetables featured in this chapter are, for the most part, in season in summer, when most block parties and barbecues take place. You'll find recipes for all seasons sprinkled throughout the book. The following list will help you choose the recipes that best fit the season.

- **FALL:** Apples, broccoli, Brussels sprouts, butternut squash, cauliflower, grapes, pears, pomegranates, potatoes, and sweet potatoes

- **WINTER:** Cabbage, citrus, kale, parsnips, turnips

- **SPRING:** Artichokes, asparagus, new potatoes, peas, radishes, rhubarb, spinach, strawberries

- **SUMMER:** Arugula, basil, berries, bell peppers, corn, cucumber, eggplant melon, stone fruit, summer squash, Swiss chard, and tomatoes

Cucumber and Potato Salad with Mustard-Dill Vinaigrette

Prep time: 10 minutes
Total time: 25 minutes
Serves 8

Move over, mayo-drenched potato salad. The mustard-dill vinaigrette makes this a light, fresh-tasting rendition of a barbecue classic. Tossing the potatoes in the vinaigrette while they are still warm allows the flavors of the vinaigrette to penetrate the potatoes more readily.

2½ pounds baby red potatoes

2 tablespoons whole-grain mustard

2 tablespoons red wine vinegar

¼ cup extra-virgin olive oil

1¼ teaspoons kosher salt

¼ teaspoon freshly ground black pepper

3 Kirby or 1 hothouse cucumber, quartered lengthwise and sliced

6 scallions (white and light green parts), thinly sliced

½ cup loosely packed fresh dill, chopped

Place the potatoes in a large pot, cover with cold water, and bring to a boil. Add a large pinch of salt, decrease the heat, and simmer until the potatoes are tender when pierced with a paring knife, 15 to 18 minutes. Drain and run under cold water to cool, then cut into quarters.

In a large bowl, whisk together the mustard, vinegar, oil, salt, and pepper. Add the potatoes, cucumbers, scallions, and dill, and toss to combine. Refrigerate in an airtight container for up to 2 days.

COOK'S TIP: Be sure to check the salad for seasoning before serving, as the potatoes tend to absorb and neutralize salt the longer they sit.

Grilled Zucchini and Eggplant Salad with Basil

Prep time: 25 minutes
Total time: 25 minutes
Serves 6 to 8

This is the ultimate summer garden salad, with little need for seasoning other than the smokiness of the grill. Zucchini and eggplant fresh from your local farmer's market will make this salad all the more vibrant.

8 medium zucchini (about 2½ pounds), sliced lengthwise ¼ inch thick

1 medium eggplant, sliced into ¼-inch-thick rounds

¼ cup plus 1 tablespoon extra-virgin olive oil

2 cups loosely packed fresh basil leaves, torn

1 teaspoon kosher salt

¼ teaspoon crushed red pepper

Heat the grill to medium-high. Grill the zucchini (without oil) until tender and slightly charred, 3 to 4 minutes per side. Transfer to a large bowl. Brush the eggplant with ¼ cup of the oil and grill until charred and tender, 3 to 4 minutes per side. Add to the bowl of zucchini.

Gently toss the zucchini and eggplant with the basil, salt, red pepper, and the remaining 1 tablespoon oil. Serve warm or at room temperature.

COOK'S TIP: This salad is best served the same day it is made, but if you find yourself with leftovers, do yourself a favor and put them on a sandwich of a warm baguette with sliced fresh mozzarella.

Summer Corn Salad with Chiles, Lime, and Feta

Prep time: 10 minutes
Total time: 10 minutes
Serves 6 to 8

Nothing is better than fresh, sweet corn cut straight from the cob, no cooking necessary. Hold each ear of corn right in the mixing bowl to cut off the kernels, so that you will catch the corn milk as well as the kernels. Fresh lime juice and feta cheese give a contemporary kick to this super-quick, no-cook summer staple.

8 cups fresh corn kernels (from 8 to 10 ears)

1 cup loosely packed fresh cilantro, chopped

½ medium red onion, chopped

2 jalapeño chiles, seeded and thinly sliced into half-moons

¼ cup olive oil

3 tablespoons freshly squeezed lime juice (from about 2 limes)

1 teaspoon kosher salt

¼ teaspoon freshly ground black pepper

1 cup (4 ounces) crumbled feta cheese

In a large bowl, combine the corn kernels, cilantro, onion, jalapeños, oil, lime juice, salt, and pepper. Gently fold in the feta.

COOK'S TIP: The best way to choose corn is to pull back the green husks and look for tightly packed, firm corn kernels. Store fresh corn in the refrigerator, unshucked, for up to 3 days; after that the corn kernels will become starchy.

Prosciutto and Melon with Mozzarella and Mint

Prep time: 10 minutes
Total time: 10 minutes
Serves 6 to 8

Arranging beautiful ingredients on a platter is as easy as it is impressive. Simply let the ingredients do the work for you.

12 ounces thinly sliced prosciutto

1 small ripe cantaloupe, seeded

1 pound bocconcini (small fresh mozzarella balls)

1 cup fresh mint leaves

2 tablespoons extra-virgin olive oil

¼ teaspoon kosher salt

¼ teaspoon freshly ground black pepper

Arrange the prosciutto in a layer on a large platter. Using a small spoon or melon baller, scoop out bite-size pieces of cantaloupe and arrange them over the prosciutto. Top with the bocconcini, and sprinkle with the mint. Drizzle with the oil and season with the salt and pepper.

COOK'S TIP: *Prosciutto* is the Italian word for "ham," but to us it means "dry-cured ham" and "delicious." Look for imported prosciutto from Parma or San Daniele, and make sure your butcher slices it paper-thin.

Platter of Tomatoes with Pepperoncini Vinaigrette

Prep time: 10 minutes
Total time: 10 minutes
Serves 6 to 8

The heat and brine of pepperoncini chiles add an edge to one of summer's most popular garden veggies. Bold blue cheese intensifies the flavor.

4 pounds beefsteak or heirloom tomatoes, sliced

1 cup (4 ounces) crumbled blue cheese

½ cup pepperoncini, chopped

¼ cup freshly squeezed lemon juice

¼ cup extra-virgin olive oil

¾ teaspoon kosher salt

¼ teaspoon freshly ground black pepper

1 cup loosely packed fresh basil leaves

Arrange the tomatoes on a large platter, and scatter with the blue cheese.

In a small bowl, combine the pepperoncini, lemon juice, oil, salt, and pepper, and drizzle over the tomatoes. Scatter the basil leaves over the top.

COOK'S TIP: Select tomatoes that actually smell like tomatoes, have a deep color, and have a slight give to them when squeezed. Store tomatoes, stem side up, at room temperature, not in the refrigerator.

Thai Watermelon and Shrimp Salad

Prep time: 20 minutes
Total time: 20 minutes
Serves 8

The kick of ginger combined with the cool essence of mint may just make this effervescent watermelon salad the star attraction of your barbecue.

1 pound peeled and deveined medium shrimp, tails removed

6 cups 1-inch watermelon pieces (from about 2 pounds)

6 scallions (white and light green parts), thinly sliced

½ cup loosely packed fresh basil leaves, torn

¼ cup loosely packed fresh mint, torn

2 tablespoons olive oil

2 tablespoons freshly squeezed lime juice (from 1 lime)

1 tablespoon grated fresh ginger

¾ teaspoon kosher salt

¼ teaspoon freshly ground black pepper

Bring a large pot of salted water to a boil. Add the shrimp and cook until opaque throughout, 2 to 3 minutes. With a slotted spoon, transfer the shrimp to a bowl of ice water to stop the cooking, then drain.

In a large bowl, combine the watermelon, scallions, basil, mint, oil, lime juice, ginger, salt, and pepper. Gently fold in the shrimp.

COOK'S TIP: You can poach the shrimp 1 day in advance, but it is best to assemble this salad just before serving, as the lime juice and ginger can "overcook" the shrimp and make them mealy.

Romaine Salad with Salami, Mozzarella, and Peppadew Peppers

Prep time: 10 minutes
Total time: 10 minutes
Serves 8

Imported from South Africa, the red, pickled peppadew pepper is tangy and sweet with a mild heat, a delightful complement to this crisp, cool salad. Pickled cherry peppers are a slightly spicier substitute.

2 large heads romaine lettuce, cut crosswise into 1-inch strips

1 pound fresh mozzarella cheese, cut into ½-inch pieces

½ small cured sausage, such as salami or soppressata, sliced (about 2 cups)

1 cup peppadew peppers, quartered

1 cup loosely packed fresh flat-leaf parsley leaves

3 tablespoons extra-virgin olive oil

1 tablespoon red wine vinegar

½ teaspoon kosher salt

¼ teaspoon freshly ground black pepper

In a large bowl, combine the lettuce, mozzarella, sausage, peppadews, parsley, oil, vinegar, salt, and pepper.

COOK'S TIP: Select small whole salami and slice it yourself. That way you get bite-size pieces rather than the large rounds from the deli counter.

Grilled Corn on the Cob with Chipotle and Parsley Butters

Prep time: 15 minutes
Total time: 25 minutes
Serves 8

Chipotle and parsley butters liven up standard corn on the cob. Try these butters on grilled steak and chicken, too.

8 ears fresh corn

1 cup (2 sticks) unsalted butter, at room temperature

¼ cup (1 ounce) grated Parmesan cheese

2 teaspoons freshly squeezed lime juice

¼ teaspoon ground chipotle pepper

1 teaspoon kosher salt

½ cup loosely packed fresh flat-leaf parsley, chopped

Heat the grill to medium-high.

Peel back (without removing) the husks, and remove the silk from the corn. Return the husks back around the corn to cover, and soak in cold water for at least 10 minutes and up to 1 hour. Grill, turning occasionally, until the husks are charred and the corn is tender, 10 to 15 minutes.

For the chipotle butter, in a small bowl, combine ½ cup of the butter, the Parmesan, lime juice, chipotle, and ½ teaspoon of the salt.

For the parsley butter, in a small bowl, combine the remaining ½ cup butter, the parsley, and the remaining ½ teaspoon of salt.

Serve the corn with the butters.

COOK'S TIP: Wrap the butters tightly with plastic wrap and refrigerate for up to 1 week. Or, for easy slicing, shape the butters into logs, wrap tightly with plastic wrap, and freeze before using (for up to 1 month).

Putting Your Extra Herbs to Work

Wondering what to do with your leftover bunch of rosemary or thyme after you've used the small amount that's often needed in a recipe? Here are a few ideas for making good use of fresh herbs.

- Make a dip for bread or a sauce for steak or chicken by stirring chopped herbs, chopped garlic, and a splash of balsamic vinegar into olive oil.

- Toss the herbs into soup, salad, or pasta.

- For soft herbs (such as basil, cilantro, or parsley), make a quick pesto: Puree the herbs in a food processor with olive oil, nuts (pine nuts or walnuts), grated Parmesan, salt, and pepper. This type of pesto freezes well.

- Add a fresh herb sprig to iced tea, lemonade, or your favorite cocktail.

Pepper Jack Chicken Enchiladas with Tomatillo Sauce

Prep time: 1 hour
Total time: 1 hour 20 minutes
Serves 8

Inside their papery skins, tomatillos resemble small green tomatoes, and they have a tasty, tart flavor. Blended with jalapeños, cilantro, and cream, they add a distinct and wonderful flair to these chicken- and veggie-packed enchiladas. But if tomatillos aren't available and time is a factor, store-bought green enchilada sauce is a fine substitution for the tomatillo sauce. Using a rotisserie chicken will trim the prep time, too.

Sauce

1 tablespoon olive oil

1 medium yellow onion

2 cloves garlic, smashed

1 teaspoon kosher salt

2 pounds tomatillos, husked

4 jalapeño chiles, halved and seeded

1 cup low-sodium chicken broth

2 cups loosely packed fresh cilantro

1 cup heavy cream

For the sauce, heat the oil in a large saucepan over medium-high heat. Add the onion, garlic, and ½ teaspoon of the salt and cook, stirring often, until beginning to soften, 5 to 6 minutes. Add the tomatillos, jalapeños, and chicken broth and simmer, covered, until the tomatillos are tender, about 10 minutes. Using a blender or immersion blender, puree the mixture with the cilantro until smooth. Stir in the cream and the remaining ½ teaspoon salt.

For the filling, place the chicken in a large pot with enough cold water to cover and a large pinch of salt and bring to a boil. Decrease the heat and gently simmer until cooked through, 20 to 25 minutes; transfer to a plate. Once cool enough to handle, shred the chicken into a large bowl.

Preheat the oven to 375°F.

Filling

4 bone-in chicken breast halves (about 3 pounds)

1 tablespoon olive oil

1 medium red onion, chopped

3 medium zucchini (about 1 pound), quartered lengthwise and sliced

3 cups fresh corn kernels (from 3 ears)

1 cup (4 ounces) grated pepper Jack cheese

1 cup (4 ounces) grated Monterey Jack cheese, plus more for sprinkling

¾ teaspoon kosher salt

¼ teaspoon freshly ground black pepper

16 (8-inch) flour tortillas

Meanwhile, heat the oil in a large skillet over medium-high heat. Add the onion and cook, stirring, until beginning to soften, 3 to 4 minutes. Add the zucchini and cook, stirring, until tender, about 5 minutes. Transfer the mixture to the bowl with the chicken. Stir in the corn, cheeses, salt, and pepper. Divide the mixture among the tortillas and roll up.

Spread a thin layer of the sauce into two 9 by 13-inch baking pans. Add the enchiladas, seam side down, to the pan. Cover with the remaining sauce and sprinkle with more cheese. Bake until heated through, about 20 minutes.

COOK'S TIP: Refrigerate the filling and sauce separately in airtight containers for up to 2 days, then assemble. Or assemble the enchiladas and the sauce in the baking pan, wrap tightly with aluminum foil, and freeze for up to 2 months. Bake directly from the freezer, covered with foil, until heated through, 40 to 50 minutes.

Spiced Coffee–Rubbed Baby Back Ribs

Prep time: 10 minutes
Total time: 40 minutes
Serves 8

The coffee-infused barbecue spice rub gives ribs an unexpected flair that will make your guests say "Wow!" The beauty of a rub is that it adds a last-minute punch of flavor to meat and poultry when you don't have time to marinate. Experiment with the spices and dried herbs in your spice drawer, like ground cumin, chipotle powder, and dried oregano, and customize your own spice rub to your liking.

6 cloves garlic, chopped

¼ cup firmly packed dark brown sugar

¼ cup chili powder

1 tablespoon ground instant espresso powder

1 tablespoon kosher salt

2 teaspoons freshly ground black pepper

2 teaspoons ground mustard

1 teaspoon cayenne pepper

6 pounds baby back ribs (about 3 racks)

Heat the grill to medium.

In a small bowl, combine the garlic, sugar, chili powder, espresso, salt, black pepper, mustard, and cayenne. Rub evenly over the ribs.

Grill the ribs, covered, turning occasionally, until cooked through, 30 to 35 minutes. Transfer to a cutting board and let rest for 5 minutes before slicing.

||||||||||||||||||||||||||||||||||||||||||||||||||||||||||||||||||||||||||||||||||||||||||||||||||||||||||

COOK'S TIP: Coat the ribs with the spice rub up to 24 hours in advance and deliver them ready to grill, or grill up to 4 hours in advance. These ribs are delicious at room temperature.

Soy-Ginger Chicken Drumsticks

Prep time: 10 minutes
Total time: 1 hour 40 minutes (includes marinating time)
Serves 8

Who needs a knife and fork? These richly flavored, kid-friendly drumsticks are delicious hot off the grill, at room temperature, or chilled—perfect whether you're grilling at home or heading to a party. The longer they marinate, the better. You may want to double this recipe, since the drumsticks are guaranteed to go quickly.

½ cup low-sodium soy sauce

3 tablespoons grated fresh ginger

¼ cup firmly packed dark brown sugar

1 tablespoon chili-garlic sauce (found in the Asian section of your grocery store)

16 chicken drumsticks

In a large resealable plastic bag, combine the soy sauce, ginger, sugar, and chili-garlic sauce. Add the chicken and let marinate, refrigerated, for at least 1 hour and up to 24 hours, occasionally turning the bag to ensure even marinating.

Heat the grill to medium. Discard the marinade and grill the chicken, covered, turning occasionally, until cooked through, 30 to 35 minutes.

||||||||||||||||||||||||||||||||||||||||||||||||||||||||||||||||||||||||||||||||||||||||||||||||||||||||||

COOK'S TIP: Grilling chicken, whether by direct or indirect methods, over medium heat ensures an evenly cooked, moist, tender chicken with a crispy skin. For added spice, try using the leftover chili-garlic sauce in other marinades or Asian vinaigrettes, spoon over Pad Thai, or stir into scrambled eggs the last minute of cooking (be careful, a little goes a long way).

Lemon-Thyme Chicken Skewers

Prep time: 15 minutes
Total time: 1 hour (includes marinating time)
Serves 8

Skewers are the ultimate cookout food—easy to eat one-handed while you stand and chat. Pair these chicken skewers with skewered vegetables such as zucchini, eggplant, bell peppers, and onions. Simply brush with oil, season with salt and pepper, and then grill until tender.

¼ cup olive oil

4 cloves garlic, chopped

2 tablespoons fresh thyme leaves

2 teaspoons grated lemon zest

1 teaspoon kosher salt

½ teaspoon freshly ground black pepper

4 pounds boneless, skinless chicken breasts, cut into 2-inch pieces

In a resealable plastic bag, combine the oil, garlic, thyme, lemon zest, salt, and pepper.

Thread the chicken pieces onto sixteen 8-inch skewers, add to the bag, and let marinate in the refrigerator for at least 30 minutes and up to 4 hours.

Heat the grill to medium. Grill the chicken, turning occasionally, until cooked through, 12 to 15 minutes.

Chocolate-Pecan Sheet Cake

Prep time: 20 minutes
Total time: 40 minutes
Serves 20

You can be out of the house in less than 45 minutes with this freshly baked, frost-while-still-warm, old-fashioned sheet cake.

1 cup pecan halves

1½ cups (3 sticks) unsalted butter

2 cups all-purpose flour, spooned and leveled

1¾ cups firmly packed dark brown sugar

½ cup plus ⅓ cup unsweetened cocoa powder

1¼ teaspoons baking soda

¾ teaspoon kosher salt

½ cup sour cream

1 teaspoon pure vanilla extract

2 large eggs

½ cup heavy cream

3 cups confectioners' sugar

COOK'S TIP: Store tightly covered with plastic wrap or aluminum foil for up to 4 days.

Preheat the oven to 350°F. Butter and flour a 17¼ by 11½ by 1-inch baking sheet, tapping out the excess flour.

Place the pecans on a separate baking sheet and bake until toasted and fragrant, 8 to 10 minutes. When cool enough to handle, coarsely chop.

In a small saucepan over medium heat, melt 2 sticks of the butter along with 1 cup water.

In a large bowl, whisk together the flour, sugar, ½ cup of the cocoa powder, baking soda, and ½ teaspoon of the salt. Add the butter mixture and mix until smooth. Mix in the sour cream and vanilla, then the eggs, one at a time, until just combined. Pour into the prepared baking sheet and bake until a toothpick inserted in the center comes out with a few moist crumbs attached, 15 to 18 minutes. Let cool for 5 minutes on a wire rack.

Meanwhile, using the same saucepan that you melted the butter in (no need to wash), melt the heavy cream and the remaining 1 stick butter.

In a large bowl, whisk together the confectioners' sugar and the remaining ⅓ cup of cocoa powder and ¼ teaspoon of salt. Add the butter-cream mixture, whisking until smooth. Stir in the toasted pecans and spread the frosting evenly over the warm cake.

Right-Side-Up Peach Cake

Prep time: 20 minutes
Total time: 2 hours (includes cooling time)
Serves 8

What's summer without juicy peaches? You also can use this scrumptious, moist buttermilk cake as the base for experimenting with other stone fruit: Try it with 4 to 6 apricots, 3 to 4 nectarines, or 4 to 6 plums.

1½ cups all-purpose flour, spooned and leveled

¾ teaspoon baking powder

¼ teaspoon baking soda

¼ teaspoon kosher salt

10 tablespoons (1¼ sticks) unsalted butter, at room temperature

1¼ cups plus 1 tablespoon sugar

2 large eggs

1 teaspoon pure vanilla extract

⅔ cup buttermilk

3 to 4 ripe peaches, cut into ¼-inch wedges

Preheat the oven to 350°F. Butter and flour a 9-inch round baking pan, tapping out the excess flour, and line the bottom with parchment paper, or butter and flour a 9-inch springform pan.

In a medium bowl, whisk together the flour, baking powder, baking soda, and salt.

Working with a stand mixer, preferably fitted with the paddle attachment, or with a hand mixer with a large bowl, beat the butter and 1¼ cups of the sugar on medium speed until fluffy. Beat in the eggs, one at a time, and add the vanilla. With the mixer on low speed, alternately add one-third of the flour mixture and half of the buttermilk, scraping down the sides as necessary; repeat once more, ending with the flour mixture (do not overmix).

Scrape the batter evenly into the prepared pan. Arrange the peaches in a single layer of concentric circles, starting from the outside and working your way in, over the top of the batter.

Sprinkle with the remaining 1 tablespoon sugar. Bake until a toothpick inserted into the center comes out with a few moist crumbs attached, 40 to 45 minutes. Let cool on a wire rack for at least 1 hour before unmolding.

If using a cake pan, invert the cake onto a plate, remove the parchment, and invert again to serve the cake top side up. For the springform pan, remove the ring and use a spatula to slide the cake onto a plate.

COOK'S TIP: This cake will retain its moistness, tightly wrapped and refrigerated, for up to 3 days.

Blueberry-Blackberry Cobbler

Prep time: 20 minutes
Total time: 1 hour 5 minutes
Serves 6 to 8

This simple, biscuit-topped cobbler has a fresh berry blend that is irresistibly both tart and sweet. Look for berries that are deeply colored, firm and plump, and popping with sweet juice. It's always best to sample one, if you can, before you buy.

6 cups blackberries

2 cups blueberries

⅓ cup plus ¼ cup sugar

1½ cups plus 2 tablespoons all-purpose flour, spooned and leveled

2 teaspoons baking powder

½ teaspoon kosher salt

6 tablespoons (¾ stick) cold unsalted butter, cut into small pieces

1 cup heavy cream

Preheat the oven to 375°F.

In a large bowl, gently toss the blackberries, blueberries, ⅓ cup of the sugar, and 2 tablespoons of the flour. Transfer to a shallow 2- to 3-quart baking dish.

In a separate bowl, whisk together the baking powder, salt, and the remaining ¼ cup sugar and 1½ cups flour. With a pastry blender or your fingers, cut in the butter until coarse, irregular crumbs form. Stir in the cream until just combined (it will be like a moist biscuit dough). Scoop and place the dough, large spoonfuls at a time, over the top of the berries. Place the baking dish on a baking sheet and bake until the top is golden, 40 to 45 minutes. Let cool on a wire rack.

COOK'S TIP: Be sure to use a shallow baking dish that gives you the most surface area for your cobbler top. This dessert is best served the same day it is made, either warm or at room temperature.

Peanut Butter Chip Chocolate Cookies

Prep time: 20 minutes
Total time: 40 minutes
Makes 48 cookies

Peanut butter and chocolate is, of course, the ultimate indulgence. These cakelike cookies are best when ever-so-slightly underbaked.

2 cups all-purpose flour, spooned and leveled

1 cup unsweetened cocoa powder

2 teaspoons baking powder

½ teaspoon kosher salt

2 sticks (1 cup) unsalted butter, at room temperature

1½ cups sugar

2 large eggs

3⅓ cups (two 10-ounce packages) peanut butter chips

Preheat the oven to 350°F. Line 2 baking sheets with parchment paper.

In a medium bowl, whisk together the flour, cocoa, baking powder, and salt.

Working with a stand mixer, preferably fitted with the paddle attachment, or with a hand mixer with a large bowl, beat the butter and sugar on medium speed until fluffy. Beat in the eggs, one at a time. With the mixer on low speed, mix in the flour mixture until just combined (the batter will be very stiff). Stir in the peanut butter chips.

Drop heaping tablespoon–size mounds of the batter 2 inches apart on the prepared baking sheets. Bake until firm around the edges but still soft in the middle, 10 to 12 minutes. Let cool for 5 minutes on the baking sheets before transferring the cookies to wire racks.

COOK'S TIP: Store in an airtight container for up to 2 days. Or freeze in portioned mounds for up to 1 month. Bake directly from the freezer for 12 to 15 minutes.

CHAPTER 5

MEET AND EAT

Community, Religious, and Business Gatherings

Breakfast Entrées

- Gruyère and Arugula Scrambled Egg Roll-Ups
- Sliced Egg, Radish, and Caper Baguettes
- Fresh Raspberry–Ricotta Tart
- Golden Raisin–Rosemary Scones

Light Fare

- Crustless Spinach Quiche
- Tuna and Cannellini Bean Salad with Cucumbers and Olives
- Crispy Apple and Chicken Salad with Blue Cheese and Basil
- Cold Sesame Noodle Salad
- Tomato and Oregano Flatbread
- Three Modern Sandwiches

Sweet Treats

- Olive Oil and Cornmeal Cake
- Spiced Pumpkin–Walnut Bread
- Coconut-Almond Haystacks
- Crunchy Milk Chocolate Oatmeal Bars

It's a fact: You don't go to Chicago for the weather, and you don't go to church board meetings for the food. Business breakfasts, PTA meetings, neighborhood association gatherings—these are the events where you fill up on store-bought cookies and Danish pastries that belong in a wax museum. Even when you've made a last-minute supermarket run yourself, it's always disappointing to arrive at the meeting and discover that everyone else did the same.

Here's an idea: While you're strategizing, deliberating, organizing, and (on occasion) trying to stay awake at your next meeting, why not enjoy rustic Tomato and Oregano Flatbread (page 122) or Fresh Raspberry–Ricotta Tart (page 116)? You may have no control over a lackluster agenda or an interminable budget report, but you absolutely can perk up the food.

This chapter helps you brighten a meeting with freshly made finger foods, sweet treats, and satisfying breakfast entrées. All the recipes here are exceptionally easy; the majority of them require just 10 minutes of prep time. Enough with stale bagels! Your colleagues will be amazed when you arrive for the 7 a.m. PowerPoint presentation with a platter of Gruyère and Arugula Scrambled Egg Roll-Ups (page 114). Or, for your next meeting, take prefab crudité platters off the agenda and show up with Chopped Chickpea, Parsley, and Pepper Salad Sandwiches (page 123). The vote in favor will be unanimous.

Gruyère and Arugula Scrambled Egg Roll-Ups

Prep time: 20 minutes
Total time: 20 minutes
Serves 8

This is a breakfast you can really sink your teeth into, spiked with the rich, slightly salty goodness of melted Gruyère and the peppery bite of arugula. It's an inspired choice when you're able to cook shortly before your get-together.

12 large eggs, beaten

½ teaspoon kosher salt

¼ teaspoon freshly ground
  black pepper

1 tablespoon unsalted butter

4 scallions (white and light green
  parts), chopped

4 cups loosely packed arugula,
  coarsely chopped

1 cup grated Gruyère or Swiss
  cheese

¼ cup loosely packed fresh dill,
  chopped

8 (8-inch) flour tortillas, warmed

In a medium bowl, combine the eggs, 2 tablespoons water, salt, and pepper.

Melt the butter in a large nonstick skillet over medium heat. Cook the scallions until softened, 1 to 2 minutes. Pour in the eggs and scramble until they just begin to set. Add the arugula, cheese, and dill and scramble until the eggs are set and the cheese is melted (do not over-scramble).

Divide the eggs among the tortillas. Fold over the opposing ends of each tortilla to help seal in the eggs and roll up like a burrito.

Wrap each roll-up in aluminum foil to keep warm for transport.

Sliced Egg, Radish, and Caper Baguettes

Prep time: 10 minutes
Total time: 25 minutes
Serves 8

Eggs are so versatile that virtually any veggies will make this breakfast sandwich a meal. There's no need for a special trip to the store—use what you have. Cucumbers, asparagus, and herbs also will do the trick.

12 large eggs

2 baguettes (about 20 inches each)

¼ cup mayonnaise

10 radishes, thinly sliced

¼ cup capers

¼ teaspoon kosher salt

½ teaspoon freshly ground black pepper

Place the eggs in a large saucepan and cover with cold water. Bring to a gentle boil, remove from the heat, cover, and let stand for 12 minutes. Transfer the eggs to a large bowl of ice water to stop the cooking. (This also prevents that green edge from forming on the yolks.) Once the eggs are cool, peel and thinly slice.

Slice each baguette in half horizontally. Spread the bottom halves with mayonnaise, then layer with the eggs, radishes, and capers; season with the salt and pepper. Top with the top halves of the baguettes and cut each baguette into 4 sandwiches.

COOK'S TIP: Hard-boiled eggs are the ultimate make-ahead protein. You can store them for up to 1 week, unpeeled, in the refrigerator.

Fresh Raspberry–Ricotta Tart

Prep time: 10 minutes
Total time: 35 minutes
Serves 8

This is a riff on the cheese Danish, but much easier, to say the least, and tastier because the fruit is fresh. Any fresh berry will work.

1 sheet frozen puff pastry (from a 17.25-ounce package), thawed

½ cup ricotta cheese

2 tablespoons sugar, plus more for sprinkling

½ teaspoon grated lemon zest

1½ cups fresh raspberries (about 6 ounces)

Preheat the oven to 400°F. Line a baking sheet with parchment paper.

Lay the pastry flat on a work surface and cut in half to make 2 rectangles. Place on the baking sheet. Score a ½-inch border around each rectangle without cutting all the way through the pastry.

In a small bowl, combine the ricotta, 2 tablespoons of the sugar, and the lemon zest. Spread the ricotta mixture within the borders of each pastry and top with the raspberries. Sprinkle the borders with more sugar. Bake until the edges are golden and crisp, about 25 minutes. Serve at room temperature or chilled. This pastry is best enjoyed the same day it is made.

Golden Raisin–Rosemary Scones

Prep time: 15 minutes
Total time: 30 minutes
Makes 8 scones

This recipe is a snap to make, all satisfyingly done by hand. The piney scent of rosemary is an unexpected and welcome surprise in the morning. If you're not crazy for raisins, currants or chopped dried apricots are the perfect substitution.

2 cups all-purpose flour, spooned and leveled

⅓ cup sugar

1 tablespoon baking powder

½ teaspoon kosher salt

6 tablespoons (¾ stick) chilled unsalted butter, cut into small pieces

¾ cup heavy cream, plus 1 tablespoon for brushing

½ cup golden raisins

2 teaspoons chopped fresh rosemary

Preheat the oven to 400°F. Line a baking sheet with parchment paper.

In a medium bowl, whisk together the flour, sugar, baking powder, and salt. Cut in the butter with a pastry blender or your fingers until coarse, irregular crumbs form. Stir in ¾ cup of the cream until just combined and the dough holds together when squeezed (add an extra tablespoon or two of cream if the dough seems too dry). Stir in the raisins and rosemary.

Turn the dough onto a floured work surface and gently knead a few times until the dough comes together. Shape into a ¾-inch-thick disk. Cut into 8 wedges and place on the prepared baking sheet. Brush the tops with the remaining 1 tablespoon cream. Bake until the edges are golden, 15 to 17 minutes. Let cool on a wire rack.

|||||||||||||||||||||||||||||||||||||||||||||||||||||||||||||||||||||||||||||||||||||||||||||||||||||||||

COOK'S TIP: Store in an airtight container for up to 2 days or tightly wrap the portioned dough and freeze for up to 1 month. Bake directly from the freezer for 18 to 20 minutes.

Crustless Spinach Quiche

Prep time: 10 minutes
Total time: 55 minutes
Serves 6 to 8

Packed with spinach and bolstered by eggs, this savory quiche is nutritious and satisfying, an ideal choice for a long meeting that overlaps with mealtime. Because it's crustless, the quiche is super-quick to make and easy to serve as a finger food. No crumbs!

8 large eggs, beaten

1½ cups whole milk

1 cup (4 ounces) grated Gruyère or Swiss cheese

1 (1-pound) package frozen chopped spinach, thawed

Pinch of freshly grated nutmeg

½ teaspoon kosher salt

¼ teaspoon freshly ground black pepper

Preheat the oven to 375°F. Butter a 9- or 10-inch pie plate.

In a large bowl, combine the eggs, milk, and cheese. Squeeze the spinach of any excess water and stir into the eggs along with the nutmeg, salt, and pepper. Pour the mixture into the prepared pie plate and bake until puffed and the center is just set, about 45 minutes. Slice the quiche into wedges or squares and serve warm, at room temperature, or chilled.

COOK'S TIP: A quick way to thaw frozen spinach is to place it in a colander and run it under hot water. Be sure to squeeze out all of the excess water.

Tuna and Cannellini Bean Salad with Cucumbers and Olives

Prep time: 15 minutes
Total time: 15 minutes
Serves 6 to 8

Crunchy, colorful, and bursting with flavor, this lively take on tuna will erase those school-lunchroom memories of warm, mayo-laden tuna sandwiches. Served atop a slice of baguette, it's the grown-up version of tuna salad.

1 (15-ounce) can cannellini beans, rinsed and drained

3 Kirby or 1 hothouse cucumber, quartered lengthwise and thinly sliced

½ of a medium red onion, halved and thinly sliced

½ cup pitted Kalamata olives, halved

½ cup loosely packed fresh flat-leaf parsley, chopped

2 (6-ounce) cans solid albacore tuna, drained

2 tablespoons extra-virgin olive oil

2 tablespoons red wine vinegar

½ teaspoon kosher salt

¼ teaspoon freshly ground black pepper

1 baguette (about 20 inches), thinly sliced on the diagonal

In a large bowl, combine the beans, cucumbers, onion, olives, and parsley. Add the tuna in large chunks to the bowl. Drizzle with the oil and vinegar and sprinkle with the salt and pepper. Gently toss and serve with the sliced baguette.

COOK'S TIP: Try canned tuna packed in olive oil rather than water for a tastier, richer flavor. No matter which kind you use, though, be sure to drain it before using.

Crispy Apple and Chicken Salad with Blue Cheese and Basil

Prep time: 10 minutes
Total time: 30 minutes
Serves 6 to 8

This dazzling salad can be as seasonal as you want it to be. In the summer, substitute the apples with nectarines, or in the spring, use sugar snap peas and radishes. Freshly squeezed lemon juice and blue cheese give the salad extra tang.

4 (6-ounce) boneless, skinless chicken breasts

4 scallions (white and light green parts), thinly sliced

2 crisp apples (such as Granny Smith or Winesap), cut into ½-inch pieces

2 ribs celery, thinly sliced

1 cup loosely packed fresh basil leaves, torn

1 cup (4 ounces) crumbled blue cheese

3 tablespoons extra-virgin olive oil

3 tablespoons freshly squeezed lemon juice

½ teaspoon kosher salt

¼ teaspoon freshly ground black pepper

4 pita breads, halved

Place the chicken breasts in a large saucepan and cover with cold water. Bring to a gentle boil and simmer until cooked through, 8 to 10 minutes; transfer to a plate to cool.

Meanwhile, in a large bowl, combine the scallions, apples, celery, basil, and blue cheese. Cut the cooled chicken into ½-inch pieces and add to the bowl. Drizzle with the oil and lemon juice and season with the salt and pepper. Gently toss to combine. Serve with the pita.

||||||||||||||||||||||||||||||||||||||||||||||||||||||||||||||||||||||||||||||||||||||||

COOK'S TIP: Cook the chicken up to 1 day in advance, wrap tightly, and refrigerate. When ready to use, cut up the chicken and toss it with the freshly cut ingredients.

Cold Sesame Noodle Salad

Prep time: 20 minutes
Total time: 20 minutes
Serves 8

Put away that Chinese take-out menu. You're only minutes from this refreshing favorite, loaded with noodles, crisp vegetables, and a ginger-sesame dressing with a chili-garlic kick.

1 pound spaghetti

6 tablespoons toasted sesame oil

¼ cup low-sodium soy sauce

1 tablespoon grated fresh ginger

1½ teaspoons chili-garlic sauce (found in the Asian section of your grocery store)

½ teaspoon kosher salt

4 Kirby cucumbers, quartered lengthwise and sliced

4 scallions (white and light green parts), sliced

2 medium carrots, grated (1 cup)

1 cup loosely packed fresh cilantro, chopped

½ cup peanuts, chopped

Cook the pasta according to the package directions; drain and run under cold water to cool.

Meanwhile, in a small bowl, combine the oil, soy sauce, ginger, chili-garlic sauce, and salt. In a large bowl, combine the cucumbers, scallions, carrots, cilantro, and peanuts. Add the pasta and dressing and toss to combine.

COOK'S TIP: The longer this salad marinates, the better. Try to make it a day in advance; it will keep in the refrigerator for up to 4 days.

Tomato and Oregano Flatbread

Prep time: 10 minutes
Total time: 30 minutes
Serves 4 to 6

Sure, there's nothing more satisfying than a cheesy pepperoni pizza, but you usually need beer to go with it and a nap afterward. Not with this one—it's less filling and tastes great. And it requires fewer napkins, too.

1 pound frozen pizza dough, thawed

1 pound beefsteak tomatoes (about 2), thinly sliced

2 tablespoons extra-virgin olive oil

½ teaspoon dried oregano

¼ teaspoon kosher salt

¼ teaspoon freshly ground black pepper

Preheat the oven to 425°F. Oil a baking sheet or dust it with cornmeal.

Let the dough come to room temperature, about 30 minutes. Shape the dough into about a 12-inch round and place on the prepared baking sheet. Layer with the tomatoes, drizzle with the oil, and sprinkle with the oregano, salt, and pepper. Bake until the flatbread is golden and crisp, 20 to 25 minutes. Serve hot or at room temperature.

COOK'S TIP: Look for frozen pizza dough in the freezer section of your grocery store or, better still, buy a pound of dough from your local pizza joint.

Three Modern Sandwiches

No one will suspect you of stopping off at the local deli and ordering the combo #4 when you show up with any of these inventive sandwiches—two with meat, one vegetarian. Each is uniquely flavorful, with the spot-on ratio of "good stuff" to bread.

Chopped Chickpea, Parsley, and Pepper Salad Sandwich

Prep time: 15 minutes
Total time: 15 minutes
Makes 8 sandwiches

2 (15-ounce) cans chickpeas, rinsed, drained, and chopped

1 (12-ounce) jar roasted red peppers, rinsed, drained, and chopped

4 scallions (white and light green parts), thinly sliced

2 ribs celery, chopped

½ cup loosely packed fresh flat-leaf parsley, chopped

¼ cup extra-virgin olive oil

2 tablespoons red wine vinegar

½ teaspoon kosher salt

¼ teaspoon freshly ground black pepper

16 slices sourdough bread

In a medium bowl, combine the chickpeas, red peppers, scallions, celery, parsley, oil, vinegar, salt, and pepper. Divide evenly among 8 of the bread slices and top with the remaining 8 bread slices.

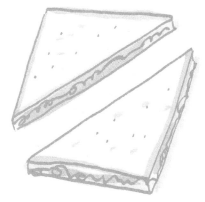

Turkey Sandwich with Cheddar, Tomato, Sprouts, and Smoked Paprika Mayonnaise

Prep time: 10 minutes
Total time: 10 minutes
Makes 8 sandwiches

½ cup mayonnaise

2 teaspoons smoked paprika

16 slices whole-grain bread

1 pound sliced deli turkey

8 ounces sharp cheddar cheese, sliced

4 medium tomatoes, thinly sliced

4 cups sprouts, such as radish or alfalfa

In a small bowl, combine the mayonnaise and paprika and spread evenly over each slice of bread. Layer the turkey, cheddar, tomatoes, and sprouts equally over 8 of the bread slices. Top with the remaining 8 bread slices.

Ham Sandwich with Caraway Cabbage Slaw and Pickles

Prep time: 15 minutes
Total time: 15 minutes
Makes 8 sandwiches

½ cup sour cream

2 tablespoons white wine vinegar

½ teaspoon caraway seeds

½ teaspoon kosher salt

⅛ teaspoon freshly ground black pepper

6 cups thinly sliced napa cabbage (from 1 small head)

1 pound sliced deli ham

4 dill pickles, thinly sliced lengthwise

16 slices marbled rye bread

In a large bowl, combine the sour cream, vinegar, caraway seeds, salt, and pepper. Add the cabbage and toss well. Layer the ham and pickles over 8 of the bread slices. Top with the slaw and then top with the remaining 8 bread slices.

Emergency Appetizers:
Three Quick-Fix Ideas
When cooking just isn't an option, you can dress up food from the store. Here's how.

- Make creative use of the salad bar. Try marinated mozzarella, olives (choose one green variety and one black), sun-dried tomatoes, and roasted peppers. Transfer them to individual bowls or attractive travel containers. Pick up a baguette or two and a big chunk of cheese, such as an aged cheddar. Bring a cutting board from home, plus serving spoons and a knife for the bread and cheese, along with plates, knives, forks, and napkins. Bamboo plates and utensils sold in grocery stores are a bit pricey but are a sustainable and nice-looking option.

- Bring an abundance of fresh, seasonal fruit. No need to spend the time slicing. Pick two types of fruit that can easily be eaten by hand, such as apples, pears, clementines, peaches, nectarines, grapes, or strawberries. What's more beautiful than a big bowl of fruit?

- Serve a pound cake with fresh raspberries and/or blueberries. Toss in a little sugar and bring some sweetened freshly whipped cream. That part you'll have to do at home.

Olive Oil and Cornmeal Cake

Prep time: 15 minutes
Total time: 1 hour 30 minutes (includes cooling time)
Serves 8

The combination of cornmeal and extra-virgin olive oil lends texture and fruitiness to this versatile cake. It's the perfect partner to coffee in the morning or strawberries and freshly whipped cream after dinner.

1 cup all-purpose flour, spooned and leveled

½ cup cornmeal

1 teaspoon baking powder

¼ teaspoon baking soda

½ teaspoon kosher salt

3 large eggs

1 cup sugar

1 (8-ounce) container crème fraîche or sour cream (about ¾ cup)

¾ cup extra-virgin olive oil

Preheat the oven to 350°F. Lightly oil and flour a 9-inch cake pan, tapping out the excess flour, and line the bottom with parchment paper, or oil and flour a 9-inch springform pan.

In a small bowl, whisk together the flour, cornmeal, baking powder, baking soda, and salt.

In a large bowl, whisk together the eggs, sugar, and crème fraîche. While whisking, slowly drizzle in the oil. Add the flour mixture and whisk until just combined (do not overmix). Scrape the batter into the prepared pan and bake until the top is golden and a toothpick inserted into the center comes out clean, 40 to 45 minutes. Let cool for at least 30 minutes on a wire rack before unmolding.

If using a cake pan, invert the cake onto a plate, remove the parchment, and invert again to serve the cake top side up. For the springform pan, remove the ring and use a spatula to slide the cake onto a plate.

Spiced Pumpkin–Walnut Bread

Prep time: 10 minutes
Total time: 1 hour 40 minutes (includes cooling time)
Serves 8 to 10

Not just for Thanksgiving pies, pumpkin puree is a handy ingredient to keep in your pantry year-round for muffins, breads, and moist cakes. Serve this easy-prep, vegan pumpkin bread for any occasion.

1¾ cups all-purpose flour, spooned and leveled

1½ teaspoons baking powder

½ teaspoon baking soda

½ teaspoon kosher salt

2 teaspoons ground cinnamon

½ teaspoon freshly grated nutmeg

1 (15-ounce can) pumpkin puree

1¼ cups sugar

½ cup canola oil

1 teaspoon pure vanilla extract

1 cup walnut halves, coarsely chopped

Preheat the oven to 350°F. Lightly oil and flour an 8½ by 4½-inch loaf pan, tapping out the excess flour.

In a small bowl, whisk together the flour, baking powder, baking soda, salt, cinnamon, and nutmeg.

In a large bowl, whisk together the pumpkin puree, sugar, oil, and vanilla. Add the flour mixture and stir until just combined. Stir in the walnuts. Scrape the batter into the pan and bake until a skewer inserted into the center comes out clean, 1 hour to 1 hour 10 minutes. Let the bread cool for 20 minutes on a wire rack before unmolding.

Store, tightly wrapped, for up to 4 days, or freeze for up to 1 month. Thaw in the refrigerator overnight.

Coconut-Almond Haystacks

Prep time: 10 minutes
Total time: 35 minutes
Makes 24 cookies

Chewy, crunchy, sweet, and easy to make, these haystacks are a crowd-pleaser for adults and kids alike. They're sure to be a big seller at your next bake sale or school carnival.

4 large egg whites

½ cup sugar

¼ teaspoon kosher salt

1 (14-ounce) package sweetened flaked coconut

1 cup sliced almonds

½ cup chocolate chips

½ cup dried apricots, coarsely chopped

Preheat the oven to 325°F. Line 2 baking sheets with parchment paper.

In a large bowl, combine the egg whites, sugar, and salt. Stir in the coconut, almonds, chocolate chips, and apricots.

Drop the mixture into golf ball–size mounds 2 inches apart on the prepared baking sheets. Bake, rotating the sheets halfway through the baking time, until the edges are golden and the cookies are set, 20 to 25 minutes. Let cool on the baking sheets for 5 minutes before transferring the haystacks to a cooling rack.

Store in an airtight container for up to 2 days.

Crunchy Milk Chocolate Oatmeal Bars

Prep time: 10 minutes
Total time: 1 hour 30 minutes (includes cooling time)
Makes 32 bars

You can never, ever go wrong with these bars: a crisp oats-and-brown-sugar crust topped with a layer of milk chocolate and chopped almonds.

2 cups old-fashioned rolled oats

1 cup firmly packed dark
   brown sugar

1 teaspoon baking soda

½ teaspoon kosher salt

½ cup (1 stick) unsalted butter,
   melted

12 ounces milk chocolate, chips or
   chopped

½ cup roasted salted almonds,
   chopped

Preheat the oven to 350°F. Butter or spray a 9 by 13-inch baking pan with nonstick cooking spray. Line the bottom of the pan with parchment paper, leaving an overhang along the long sides.

In a large bowl, combine the oats, sugar, baking soda, and salt. Stir in the butter until well combined. Press into the prepared pan and bake until bubbly and the edges begin to set, 12 to 15 minutes.

Sprinkle the chocolate evenly over the oatmeal crust and, using a spatula, smooth it out evenly. Sprinkle the nuts over the chocolate. Let cool for 30 minutes on a wire rack, then refrigerate until the chocolate is firm, about 30 minutes.

Grabbing both sides of the parchment, lift the bars out of the pan and onto a cutting board. Cut into squares.

Store in an airtight container for up to 5 days.

CHAPTER 6

Novel Ideas for

BOOK CLUBS

Dips

- Lime and Chile Crab Dip
- Smashed Peas with Manchego and Lemon
- Fresh Ricotta with Soft Herbs

Finger Foods

- Cold Poached Shrimp with Classic Cocktail Sauce
- Parmesan Palmiers
- Bacon-Wrapped Dates
- Lemon and Garlic–Marinated Mushrooms
- Rosemary- and Chili-Spiced Cashews
- Caramelized Onion, Bacon, and Blue Cheese Tart
- Zucchini Relish with Goat Cheese and Crackers
- Slow-Roasted Tomatoes and Garlic with Crostini

Sweet Treats

- Chewy Raspberry–Walnut Meringues
- Earl Grey Shortbread Cookies
- Almond-Ginger Bars
- Chocolate Chip and Candied Ginger Blondies
- Sweet Tangerine Cake

For an avid reader, nothing is more fun than a lively book club debate. Was the novel gripping, imaginative, and utterly brilliant, or was it overwrought, convoluted, and implausible? Discuss!

Still, great book discussions are only part of the draw. Most of us come for the schmoozing and the noshing, too.

Book-club food customs run the gamut. Some clubs meet for gourmet dinners provided by the host or divided among the members. One of the country's most enduring clubs, the century-old Fort Smith Women's Book Club in Arkansas, discusses nonfiction over dessert and coffee or tea served with silver and linen napkins. Some clubs plan creative meals based on the themes or setting of the month's book selection—a Chinese feast for Pearl Buck's *The Good Earth* or a menu with locally grown produce for Barbara Kingsolver's *Animal, Vegetable, Miracle*.

Yet many book clubs face a dilemma: They meet at the dinner hour on a weekday, even though the host hasn't had time to prepare a full meal, and the guests have not had time to eat dinner. For many of us, finishing the book is often challenge enough; pulling together something more elaborate than chips and dip seems an impossibility.

But it doesn't have to be. In this chapter, you'll find recipes for elegant, irresistible finger foods, like the Caramelized Onion, Bacon, and Blue Cheese Tart (page 143), which provides enough sustenance to count as dinner. When you're engrossed in a discussion, it's easy to engage in mindless munching, so we've included nutritious appetizers, such as Zucchini Relish with Goat Cheese and Crackers (page 144) and Cold Poached Shrimp with Classic Cocktail Sauce (page 137), which doesn't come with loads of guilt for overindulging. Of course, we also offer several delectable sweet treats, such as Sweet Tangerine Cake (page 150) and Earl Grey Shortbread Cookies (page 147).

For all of the compliments you'll get, the dishes in this chapter are surprisingly easy to prepare. No one needs to know that you threw them together in less time than it took to read the introduction to this month's novel.

Lime and Chile Crab Dip

Prep time: 10 minutes
Total time: 10 minutes
Serves 8

Delicate and sweet, fresh crab is always a treat. If it is not readily available to you, substitute poached chopped shrimp for an equally delicious dip. The small chopped jalapeño gives this delicate dip extra bite.

8 ounces fresh crabmeat (blue crab or Dungeness)

3 tablespoons mayonnaise

¼ teaspoon grated lime zest

1 tablespoon freshly squeezed lime juice

2 scallions (white and light green parts), chopped

1 small jalapeño chile, seeded and chopped

2 tablespoons chopped fresh tarragon

¼ teaspoon kosher salt

⅛ teaspoon freshly ground black pepper

Crackers, for serving

In a medium bowl, combine the crab, mayonnaise, lime zest, lime juice, scallions, jalapeño, tarragon, salt, and pepper. Serve with crackers.

COOK'S TIP: Be sure to pick over the crabmeat and remove any extra bits of shell and cartilage that the fishmonger may have missed.

Smashed Peas with Manchego and Lemon

Prep time: 10 minutes
Total time: 10 minutes
Serves 8

Manchego is a traditional Spanish sheep's milk cheese that ranges from mild to slightly sharp, depending on how long it has been aged. For this dip, reach for the aged (12-month) manchego, as it pairs so nicely with the sweetness of the peas. Parmesan or pecorino are good alternatives to manchego.

1 (10-ounce) package frozen peas, thawed

¾ cup (3 ounces) grated manchego cheese

2 tablespoons extra-virgin olive oil

1 tablespoon freshly squeezed lemon juice

½ teaspoon kosher salt

¼ teaspoon freshly ground black pepper

Crostini (page 145), radishes, or carrot sticks, for serving

In the bowl of a food processor, puree the peas, cheese, oil, lemon juice, salt, and pepper until almost smooth. Serve with the crostini or vegetables.

Fresh Ricotta with Soft Herbs

Prep time: 5 minutes
Total time: 5 minutes
Serves 8

Not just for lasagne, fresh ricotta is sweet, mild, and addictive. Drizzled with extra-virgin olive oil and sprinkled with a fresh herb or a mixture of herbs, it makes for the easiest, most delicious dip around.

2 cups (about 15 ounces) fresh whole-milk ricotta

1 tablespoon extra-virgin olive oil

1 tablespoon chopped fresh chives, tarragon, parsley, or basil

Pinch of kosher or sea salt and freshly ground black pepper

Crostini (page 145), radishes, or celery and/or carrot sticks, for serving

Spoon the ricotta into a serving bowl, drizzle with the oil, and sprinkle with the herbs, salt, and pepper. Serve with crostini, radishes, and/or carrots.

COOK'S TIP: If your ricotta appears to be a bit dry, mix in 2 tablespoons of heavy cream or whole milk before adding the oil and herbs.

Cold Poached Shrimp with Classic Cocktail Sauce

Prep time: 10 minutes
Total time: 10 minutes
Serves 8

Is there anything better to serve with shrimp than old-fashioned cocktail sauce? This no-fuss sauce, spiked with freshly squeezed lemon juice, is always a hit.

1½ pounds peeled and deveined large shrimp, tails left on

1 cup ketchup

2 tablespoons prepared horseradish

2 tablespoons freshly squeezed lemon juice

1 teaspoon Worcestershire sauce

Bring a large pot of salted water to a boil. Add the shrimp and cook until opaque throughout, 3 to 4 minutes. With a slotted spoon, transfer the shrimp to a bowl of ice water to stop the cooking, then drain.

In a small bowl, combine the ketchup, horseradish, lemon juice, and Worcestershire.

Serve chilled with the shrimp.

COOK'S TIP: Refrigerate the shrimp in a resealable plastic bag for up to 1 day. Refrigerate the cocktail sauce in an airtight container for up to 2 weeks.

Parmesan Palmiers

Prep time: 15 minutes
Total time: 50 minutes
Makes 42 palmiers

A sprinkling of Parmesan adds a savory twist to these classic French pastries. Light, crispy, and golden brown, they are much easier to make than their delicate appearance would suggest. Pair them with Lemon- and Garlic-Marinated Mushrooms (page 141).

2 sheets frozen puff pastry (from a 17.25-ounce package), thawed

1 large egg, beaten

1 cup (4 ounces) grated Parmesan cheese, plus more for sprinkling

¼ teaspoon kosher salt

Preheat the oven to 400°F. Line 2 baking sheets with parchment paper.

Lay 1 sheet of pastry out flat on a lightly floured work surface. Brush the pastry with half the egg and sprinkle with half the cheese and half the salt. Tightly roll one side of the pastry to the middle of the sheet, then roll the opposite side to the middle so that the two rolls meet. Repeat the procedure with the remaining pastry, egg, cheese, and salt. Freeze the rolls for 10 minutes.

Cut each log crosswise into ⅜-inch-thick slices and place the slices flat on the prepared baking sheets, 1 inch apart. Sprinkle the tops with extra cheese and bake, rotating the sheets halfway through the baking time, until crisp, 22 to 25 minutes. Let cool on wire racks.

COOK'S TIP: Puff pastry bakes best when it is very cold, so after slicing and sprinkling with cheese, pop the palmiers in the oven immediately to ensure a flaky crust. Store in an airtight container for up to 2 days.

The Art of Assembling
a Cheese Platter

When you don't have time to cook, or even when you do, a cheese platter is a lovely and simple way to make guests feel welcome. A supermarket cheese counter can be overwhelming, so here are some thoughts on what to buy.

For a party of eight or less, offer two or three cheeses, figuring about 2 ounces per type of cheese per person. Start with a bloomy cheese ("bloomy" refers to the soft, white rind), such as a buttery, rich Brie or Humboldt Fog. Add a firm, subtle cheese, such as manchego or Gruyère, and, if you like, a hard, caramelized cheese such as Parmigiano-Reggiano or an aged Gouda. Cut a few slices so that guests don't hesitate to dig in.

For eight to twelve people, offer one or two additional varieties. Try a pungent cheese such as Epoisses or Taleggio—stinky but delicious!—and a blue cheese, such as Gorgonzola or Maytag.

Supplement your cheese platter with crackers, breadsticks, olives, nuts, Italian cold cuts like salami and prosciutto, seasonal fruit, dried fruit, and/or chutney. All you need are a cheese board or platter, knives, and small bowls or plates for the accompaniments. Let the beautiful food stand on its own.

Figure three glasses of wine per person (there are four glasses of wine per 750-milliliter bottle). As with food, it's always better to have leftovers than to run out.

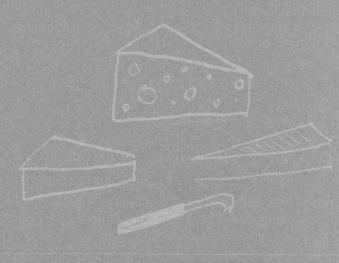

Bacon-Wrapped Dates

Prep time: 10 minutes
Total time: 25 minutes
Serves 8

Medjool dates are prized for their large size; sweet, honey-like flavor; and chewy, rich texture. Wrapped in bacon and stuffed with Parmesan cheese and a roasted almond, they make for an intensely flavorful and perfectly salty-sweet bite.

24 dates (preferably Medjool), pitted

2 ounces Parmesan cheese, cut into 24 (½-inch) pieces

24 roasted almonds

12 slices bacon, halved crosswise

Preheat the oven to 425°F.

Stuff each date with a piece of Parmesan and an almond, pressing the date together to seal. Wrap with a piece of bacon and place seam side down on a baking sheet. Bake for 6 to 8 minutes, then turn and bake for 4 to 6 minutes more, until crisp. Serve with toothpicks.

COOK'S TIP: Look for fresh dates in the produce section. Make sure they are soft and pliable; pass by the ones that look like they have started to crystallize around the edges. Store the dates in an airtight container on your counter for up to 1 week or in the refrigerator for up to 1 month.

Lemon and Garlic–Marinated Mushrooms

Prep time: 10 minutes
Total time: 40 minutes
Serves 6 to 8

Simply marinated in a toasted garlic–flavored oil with lemon and parsley, these mushrooms are delightfully light and refreshing. There's no need to stuff or bake them. Make the mushrooms a day ahead to let the flavors develop even more.

¼ cup olive oil

2 cloves garlic, sliced

¼ cup freshly squeezed lemon juice

1 teaspoon kosher salt

¼ teaspoon freshly ground black pepper

1½ pounds medium button mushrooms, quartered

½ cup loosely packed fresh flat-leaf parsley, chopped

Heat the oil in a small skillet over medium heat. Add the garlic and cook, swirling the skillet, until light golden brown, 1 to 2 minutes. Pour into a large bowl and combine with the lemon juice, salt, and pepper. Add the mushrooms and parsley and toss to coat. Let marinate in the refrigerator for at least 30 minutes and up to 12 hours. Serve with toothpicks.

COOK'S TIP: If you plan on making the mushrooms more than 2 hours in advance, toss the parsley in just before serving to preserve its color.

Rosemary- and Chili-Spiced Cashews

Prep time: 5 minutes
Total time: 5 minutes
Serves 8

Cashews are by nature addictive; seasoned with fresh rosemary, chili powder, and a touch of sugar, they may become an obsession. These nuts are easy to make ahead, so you can spend your last days before the meeting cramming to finish the book.

1 tablespoon unsalted butter

2 cups (about 10 ounces) roasted unsalted cashews

2 teaspoons sugar

1 teaspoon chopped fresh rosemary

¾ teaspoon kosher salt

½ teaspoon chili powder

Melt the butter in a medium skillet over medium heat. Add the cashews and toss to coat. Sprinkle the sugar, rosemary, salt, and chili powder over the cashews and cook, tossing, until fragrant, 2 to 3 minutes.

Let cool, then store in an airtight container for up to 2 weeks.

Caramelized Onion, Bacon, and Blue Cheese Tart

Prep time: 15 minutes
Total time: 40 minutes
Serves 8

There's nothing subtle about these tarts. The onion, bacon, and blue cheese combination is so heavenly that you will have to make a double batch. Follow them up with the Chewy Raspberry-Walnut Meringues (page 146).

4 slices bacon, cut crosswise into ½-inch-thick pieces

2 medium yellow onions, thinly sliced

¼ teaspoon freshly ground black pepper

1 sheet frozen puff pastry (from a 17.25-ounce package), thawed

½ cup (2 ounces) crumbled blue cheese

Preheat the oven to 400°F. Line a baking sheet with parchment paper.

Cook the bacon in a large skillet over medium-high heat, stirring often, until crisp, 6 to 8 minutes; transfer to paper towels to drain. Spoon off and discard all but 2 tablespoons of the bacon drippings from the skillet.

Add the onions to the skillet and cook, stirring often, until very tender and caramelized, 12 to 15 minutes (add a splash of water to the skillet, if necessary, to help release the drippings on the bottom of the skillet). Stir in the bacon and pepper.

Lay the pastry out flat on the prepared baking sheet. Spread the onion mixture over the pastry, leaving a ½-inch border, and crumble the cheese over the top.

Bake until the pastry is golden brown and crisp along the edges, 25 to 28 minutes. Transfer to a cutting board and slice into 20 squares. Serve warm or at room temperature.

COOK'S TIP: To freeze, cook the onion-bacon mixture and let cool. Assemble the tart, wrap tightly in plastic wrap and then in aluminum foil, and freeze for up to 1 month.

Unwrap and bake directly from the freezer adding a couple of extra minutes to the baking time.

Zucchini Relish with Goat Cheese and Crackers

Prep time: 20 minutes
Total time: 20 minutes
Serves 8

This is a sort of do-it-yourself crostini, with some assembly required. First, spread the goat cheese onto the crostini or sturdy crackers (as much or as little as you like), and then top with the mild relish.

2 tablespoons olive oil

¼ medium red onion, finely chopped

2 medium zucchini (about 12 ounces), cut into ¼-inch pieces

1 yellow bell pepper, cut into ¼-inch pieces

1 tablespoon fresh thyme leaves

½ teaspoon kosher salt

⅛ teaspoon freshly ground black pepper

8 ounces fresh goat cheese

Crostini (page 145) or plain crackers, for serving

Heat the oil in a large skillet over medium-high heat. Add the onion, zucchini, bell pepper, thyme, salt, and pepper and cook, stirring, until just tender, 4 to 5 minutes.

Serve at room temperature with the goat cheese and crackers.

Refrigerate the relish in an airtight container for up to 3 days.

Slow-Roasted Tomatoes and Garlic with Crostini

Prep time: 5 minutes
Total time: 45 minutes
Serves 6 to 8

Slow roasting concentrates the sweetness and flavor in the tomatoes and garlic. Simple and delicious, this dish will become your go-to appetizer.

Tomatoes

3 pints grape tomatoes

12 cloves garlic

¼ cup extra-virgin olive oil

1 tablespoon fresh thyme leaves

1 teaspoon kosher salt

¼ teaspoon freshly ground black pepper

Crostini

1 baguette (about 20 inches), thinly sliced into rounds

2 tablespoons olive oil

For the tomatoes, preheat the oven to 350°F. On a rimmed baking sheet, toss the tomatoes, garlic, oil, thyme, salt, and pepper. Roast, stirring twice, until the tomatoes burst and begin to shrivel, 35 to 40 minutes. Let cool to room temperature.

For the crostini, increase the oven temperature to 375°F. Arrange the baguette slices on a baking sheet and brush with the oil. Bake until golden and crisp, 12 to 15 minutes. Serve the crostini with the tomatoes.

COOK'S TIP: Refrigerate the tomatoes in an airtight container for up to 4 days; let them come to room temperature before serving. Store the crostini in a resealable plastic bag for up to 5 days.

Chewy Raspberry-Walnut Meringues

Prep time: 15 minutes
Total time: 50 minutes
Makes 40 cookies

Sweet and chewy, these delightful meringues are the perfect accompaniment to a Jane Austen discussion. Don't hesitate to play with the flavors by switching up the raspberry jam with apricot preserves or orange marmalade.

3 large egg whites
¾ cup sugar
1 cup walnut halves, finely chopped
1 teaspoon pure vanilla extract
½ teaspoon kosher salt
⅓ cup raspberry jam

Preheat the oven to 350°F. Line 2 baking sheets with parchment paper.

Working with a stand mixer fitted with the whisk attachment, or with a hand mixer with a large bowl, beat the egg whites on medium speed until soft peaks form. Increase the speed to high and slowly add the sugar, beating until glossy, stiff peaks form. Gently fold in the walnuts, vanilla, and salt.

Spoon heaping tablespoon–size amounts of batter 2 inches apart onto the prepared baking sheets. Spoon ¼ teaspoon of jam into the center of each cookie and bake, rotating the sheets halfway through the baking time, until lightly golden, 15 to 18 minutes. Let cool on the baking sheets before transferring the meringues to a wire rack.

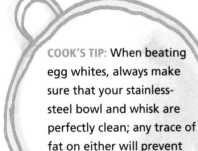

COOK'S TIP: When beating egg whites, always make sure that your stainless-steel bowl and whisk are perfectly clean; any trace of fat on either will prevent the whites from reaching their full volume.

Earl Grey Shortbread Cookies

Prep time: 20 minutes
Total time: 1 hour
Makes 28 triangle cookies

Tea isn't just for drinking. Earl Grey leaves, typically a blend of Indian and Ceylon teas, add a lovely flavor to these delicate, buttery cookies. The slightly fruity essence in the tea comes from bergamot, a Southeast Asian citrus fruit that is less tart than lemons and grown commercially in Italy.

2 cups all-purpose flour, spooned and leveled

¾ cup confectioners' sugar

½ teaspoon kosher salt

1 tablespoon Earl Grey tea leaves

1 tablespoon grated orange zest

2 sticks (1 cup) cold unsalted butter, cut into small pieces

1 teaspoon pure vanilla extract

Preheat the oven to 325°F. Line 2 baking sheets with parchment paper.

In the bowl of a food processor, pulse the flour, sugar, salt, tea leaves, and orange zest to combine. Add the butter and vanilla and pulse until the dough begins to come together. Divide the dough in half and shape into 2 disks. Wrap each disk in plastic wrap and refrigerate for 20 minutes.

On a floured surface, roll one of the disks out to a ⅜-inch-thick circle. Cut into 2-inch-wide wedges, as you would for a pie, and arrange 1 inch apart on the prepared baking sheets; repeat with the remaining dough disk. Bake, rotating the sheets halfway through the baking time, until light golden brown around the edges, 18 to 20 minutes. Let cool for 5 minutes on the baking sheets before transferring the cookies to a wire rack.

COOK'S TIP: To increase the yield of cookies, cut the dough into 2-inch squares or rounds.

Almond-Ginger Bars

Prep time: 20 minutes
Total time: 2 hours (includes cooling time)
Makes 32 squares

This almond-ginger bar was inspired by Lindsey Shere's famous almond tart recipe from Chez Panisse restaurant. With a crisp press-in crust and a ginger-infused, caramel-like filling, these bars are so heavenly that you may lose track of the book discussion.

Crust

2 cups all-purpose flour, spooned and leveled

½ cup sugar

14 tablespoons (1¾ sticks), cold unsalted butter, cut into small pieces

½ teaspoon kosher salt

Filling

1 cup heavy cream

1 cup sugar

1½ cups sliced almonds

2 teaspoons grated fresh ginger

Preheat the oven to 375°F. Butter or spray a 9 by 13-inch baking pan with nonstick cooking spray.

For the crust, in a food processor, pulse the flour, sugar, butter, and salt until crumbly and it holds together when squeezed. Using your fingers, press the dough evenly over the bottom and ½ inch up the sides of the prepared pan. Bake until lightly golden brown, 15 to 20 minutes.

Meanwhile, for the filling, in a small saucepan over medium-high heat, combine the cream and sugar; bring to a boil. Remove from the heat and stir in the almonds and ginger. Pour the mixture over the warm crust, making sure the almonds are evenly distributed.

Bake until the almonds are a light golden brown and the edges are crisp, 18 to 20 minutes. Let cool for at least 1 hour on a wire rack before slicing.

Store in an airtight container for up to 4 days.

Chocolate Chip and Candied Ginger Blondies

Prep time: 15 minutes
Total time: 2 hours (includes cooling time)
Makes 32 squares

Candied ginger adds a snappy edge to these chocolaty bars. For the most economical candied ginger, look in the bulk or nut section of your grocery store. Ginger lovers may want to cut back on the chocolate to enhance the ginger flavor.

2¼ cups all-purpose flour, spooned and leveled

1 teaspoon baking soda

½ teaspoon salt

1 cup (2 sticks) unsalted butter, at room temperature

1½ cups firmly packed dark brown sugar

1¼ cups granulated sugar

4 large eggs

2 teaspoons vanilla extract

One 12-ounce package semisweet chocolate chips

1 cup loosely packed candied ginger, chopped

Preheat the oven to 350°F. Butter or spray a 9 by 13-inch baking pan with nonstick cooking spray.

In a medium bowl, whisk together the flour, baking soda, and salt.

Working with a stand mixer, preferably fitted with the paddle attachment, or with a hand mixer with a large bowl, beat the butter, brown sugar, and granulated sugar on medium speed until fluffy, 2 to 3 minutes. Beat in the eggs, one at a time, and the vanilla. With the mixer on low speed, gradually add the flour mixture, mixing until just combined (do not overmix). Stir in the chocolate chips and ginger.

Spread the batter evenly into the prepared pan and bake until a toothpick inserted in the center comes out clean, 35 to 40 minutes. Let cool for at least 1 hour on a wire rack before slicing.

Store in an airtight container for up to 4 days.

Sweet Tangerine Cake

Prep time: 20 minutes
Total time: 1 hour 35 minutes
Serves 8

Tangerines are sweeter than oranges, with a more concentrated flavor in both the juice and the zest. Serve this single-layer cake with a dusting of confectioners' sugar or a dollop of lightly sweetened whipped cream.

1½ cups all-purpose flour, spooned and leveled

1½ teaspoons baking powder

½ teaspoon salt

12 tablespoons (1½ sticks) unsalted butter, at room temperature

1 cup granulated sugar

1 cup confectioners' sugar, plus more for dusting

3 large eggs

2 teaspoons grated tangerine or orange zest

½ cup freshly squeezed tangerine or orange juice

Preheat the oven to 350°F. Butter and flour a 9-inch round baking pan, tapping out the excess flour, and line the bottom with parchment paper, or butter and flour a 9-inch springform pan.

In a medium bowl, whisk together the flour, baking powder, and salt.

Working with a stand mixer, preferably fitted with the paddle attachment, or with a hand mixer with a large bowl, beat the butter, granulated sugar, and confectioners' sugar on medium speed until fluffy, 2 to 3 minutes. Beat in the eggs, one at a time, and the zest. With the mixer on low speed, alternately add one-third of the flour mixture and half of the juice, scraping the sides down as necessary; repeat once more, ending with the flour mixture (do not overmix). Scrape the batter evenly into the prepared pan.

COOK'S TIP: Always be careful not to overmix cake batter once the flour is added, as doing so will strengthen the glutens in the flour and result in a tough cake.

Bake until a toothpick inserted into the center comes out with a few moist crumbs attached, 40 to 45 minutes. Let cool for 30 minutes on a wire rack. If using a cake pan, invert the cake onto a plate, remove the parchment, and invert again to serve top side up. For the springform pan, remove the ring and use a spatula to slide the cake onto a plate. Let cool completely before dusting with confectioners' sugar.

CHAPTER 7

CONDOLENCES

Soups
- Smoky Corn Chowder
- Butternut Squash and Farro Soup
- Chicken Tortilla Soup

Main Dishes
- Chili-Rubbed Roast Turkey Breast and Jalapeño Cranberry Sandwiches
- Italian Sausage and White Bean Bake
- Red Wine Beef Stew
- Sweet Potato Torta
- Roasted Garlic Chicken and Root Vegetables
- Sweet Pepper and Spinach Lasagne
- Roasted Lamb with Parmesan Potatoes and Zucchini
- Chorizo, Potato, and Egg Casserole

Sweet Treats
- Banana-Hazelnut Muffins
- White Chocolate and Macadamia Nut Cookies
- Brown Sugar Swirl Coffee Cake
- Fresh Apple Cake

Each culture and faith has its own customs for the gathering after the funeral. In the South, mourners bring fried chicken and casseroles. The Jewish tradition calls for massive deli platters to descend on the home. In Minnesota, we've heard, you are not officially deceased until your relatives are in the church basement eating tuna, Jell-O salad, and Bundt cake.

Though you won't find any tuna or Jell-O recipes in this chapter, we do offer an abundance of cozy dishes to nourish and comfort the family in the days before and after the funeral. With Red Wine Beef Stew (page 162) and Smoky Corn Chowder (page 156) in the refrigerator, family members needn't worry about planning meals or providing hospitality for out-of-town guests.

We have found that cooking for a mourning family is comforting for the cook, as well. Baking Fresh Apple Cake (page 174) is a way to show your love and sympathy when you're not sure what else to do. Preparing food also helps during what may be a time of financial need; having to feed guests only adds to the household expenses. The ultimate expression of support may be organizing a meal train for the grieving family (see page 19).

Grief can last for a long time, yet the rush of meals tends to be brief. The family will no doubt be touched by an Italian Sausage and White Bean Bake (page 161) delivered a month or two after the death of a loved one, when the meals have stopped regularly arriving. The anniversary of the death might be a date to mark on your calendar for bringing a meal. (In Jewish custom, this is the day when the headstone is unveiled during a small ceremony.) Arriving at the family's home with a Sweet Pepper and Spinach Lasagne (page 166) is a special way to communicate that the loss hasn't been forgotten.

Smoky Corn Chowder

Prep time: 15 minutes
Total time: 45 minutes
Serves 6 to 8

Smoked paprika, often labeled *pimentón*, is made in Spain and packaged in an attractive tin that you can find in most supermarkets. It has the addicting smokiness that gives Spanish chorizo its characteristic flavor and is a tasty complement to corn.

2 tablespoons olive oil

2 medium yellow onions, chopped

1½ teaspoons kosher salt

2 cloves garlic, chopped

1 teaspoon smoked sweet paprika

⅛ teaspoon cayenne pepper

4 cups low-sodium chicken broth

2 cups whole milk

2 pounds Yukon Gold potatoes (about 4 medium), cut into ½-inch pieces

2 (10-ounce) packages frozen corn or 4 cups fresh corn

1 cup loosely packed fresh cilantro, chopped

¼ teaspoon freshly ground black pepper

Heat the oil in a large saucepan over medium-high heat. Add the onions and ½ teaspoon of the salt and cook, stirring often, until the onions are softened, 5 to 6 minutes. Stir in the garlic, paprika, and cayenne and cook for 1 minute.

Stir in the broth, milk, potatoes, and corn and bring to a boil. Decrease the heat and simmer until the potatoes are tender, about 20 minutes.

Using a blender or an immersion blender, puree half of the soup, then return it to the pan. Stir in the cilantro, black pepper, and the remaining 1 teaspoon salt. Reheat, if necessary.

COOK'S TIP: Frozen corn usually lacks the natural sweetness of fresh, so if you use it, stir just a pinch of sugar into the soup. Refrigerate for up to 4 days or freeze for up to 2 months.

Butternut Squash and Farro Soup

Prep time: 20 minutes
Total time: 45 minutes
Serves 6 to 8

Popular during the glory days of ancient Rome and now enjoying a revival, farro is a grain that is similar in texture to barley (but cooks in half the time, if pearled) and has a subtle, nutty flavor. If you can't easily find farro, use pearled barley instead, and increase the cooking time by 20 minutes. This soup is hearty enough for a main course, so just take along a loaf of bread and the Caesar-Like Salad (page 15).

2 tablespoons olive oil

1 medium yellow onion, chopped

1¼ teaspoons kosher salt

1 (14.5-ounce) can diced tomatoes, drained

1 small butternut squash (1½ pounds), cut into ½-inch pieces

1 cup farro

8 cups low-sodium chicken broth

¼ teaspoon freshly ground black pepper

1 cup loosely packed fresh flat-leaf parsley leaves, chopped

Heat the oil in a large saucepan over medium-high heat. Add the onion and ½ teaspoon of the salt and cook, stirring, until beginning to soften, 3 to 4 minutes. Add the tomatoes and squash and cook, stirring occasionally, for 5 minutes more. Stir in the farro, broth, pepper, and the remaining ¾ teaspoon salt and bring to a boil. Decrease the heat and simmer until the squash and farro are tender, about 20 minutes. Stir in the parsley.

‖‖‖

COOK'S TIP: With its curves, butternut squash can be tricky to peel. To make it a bit easier, first cut off the bulbous end of the squash. This will leave you with at least one straight part to peel.

Chicken Tortilla Soup

Prep time: 20 minutes
Total time: 1 hour 10 minutes
Serves 6 to 8

Rich with charred tomatoes, smoky pasilla chiles, and tortilla chips, this Mexican-inspired soup satisfies the soul. If pasilla chiles aren't readily available to you, substitute a tablespoon of chipotles in adobo sauce or a generous amount of your favorite hot sauce to ensure that you get that kick. To add an authentic, fresh feel, deliver the soup with an avocado for dicing, cilantro leaves, and limes to cut into wedges.

4 bone-in chicken breast halves (about 3 pounds)

8 cups low-sodium chicken broth

3 pasilla chiles, seeded

2 pounds (about 6) ripe medium beefsteak tomatoes, quartered

1 small white or yellow onion, cut into wedges

4 cloves garlic

1 tablespoon olive oil

¾ teaspoon kosher salt

¼ teaspoon freshly ground black pepper

8 ounces tortilla chips

1 small bunch cilantro, for serving

2 avocados, for serving

2 limes, quartered, for serving

In a large pot, place the chicken and enough chicken broth to cover (about 8 cups) and bring to a boil. Decrease the heat and simmer gently until the chicken is cooked through, 20 to 25 minutes. Transfer the chicken to a bowl and, when cool enough to handle, shred into pieces. Reserve 5 cups of the broth and refrigerate or freeze the remaining broth for another use.

Meanwhile, soak 2 of the chiles in hot water for 10 minutes; drain.

Heat the broiler. On a rimmed baking sheet, toss together the tomatoes, onion, garlic, and oil. Broil, stirring twice, until the vegetables are charred, 12 to 15 minutes. Transfer to a blender along with the soaked chiles and puree until smooth.

In a large saucepan, combine the tomato-chile mixture with the salt, pepper, and the reserved chicken broth and bring to a boil. Slice the remaining chile and stir it into the soup along with the shredded chicken.

Serve topped with crumbled chips, cilantro, avocados, and a squeeze of lime.

COOK'S TIP: Pliable and dark brown in color, the pasilla chile is the dried version of the chile chilaca and can be found in many grocery stores and Latin markets. It gives this soup its rich, smoky flavor with a bit of heat (occasionally, a hot one will slip through). To seed the chile, make a vertical slit with the tip of your knife, and remove the seeds and veins.

Chili-Rubbed Roast Turkey Breast and Jalapeño Cranberry Sandwiches

Prep time: 15 minutes
Total time: 50 minutes
Serves 8

The best part of Thanksgiving is the next day, when you get to feast on thick, juicy turkey sandwiches with homemade cranberry sauce. That's what this quick-prep dish is all about. Slice the turkey to order and serve with the cranberries and rolls for lunch or dinner sandwiches.

2 tablespoons honey

2 tablespoons olive oil

1 tablespoon chili powder

2 teaspoons dried oregano

1 teaspoon kosher salt

½ teaspoon freshly ground black pepper

1 cup plus 2 teaspoons freshly squeezed orange juice

2 (2-pound) boneless turkey breast halves

1 (12-ounce) package frozen cranberries

⅔ cup sugar

2 jalapeño chiles, seeded and thinly sliced

8 rolls or 16 slices bread of your choice

Preheat the oven to 350°F.

In a small bowl, combine the honey, oil, chili powder, oregano, salt, pepper, and 2 teaspoons of the orange juice. Rub the mixture evenly over the turkey breasts and place in a roasting pan. Roast until the internal temperature reaches 155°F, 35 to 40 minutes.

Meanwhile, in a small saucepan over medium-high heat, combine the cranberries, sugar, a pinch of salt, and the remaining 1 cup orange juice, and bring to a boil.

Lower the heat and simmer until the cranberries begin to burst and the sauce slightly thickens, 20 to 25 minutes. Stir in the jalapeños and let cool.

Slice the turkey and make sandwiches with the cranberries and rolls.

COOK'S TIP: Refrigerate the turkey, tightly wrapped, for up to 3 days and the cranberries in an airtight container for up to 5 days, or freeze for up to 1 month. Thaw in the refrigerator overnight.

Italian Sausage and White Bean Bake

Prep time: 25 minutes
Total time: 1 hour
Serves 8

This baked casserole is especially satisfying, with its combination of beans, sausage, and crispy bread crumb topping. It's also great for leftovers the next day.

3 tablespoons olive oil

1½ pounds Italian sausage, cut crosswise into 2-inch pieces

3 leeks (white and light green parts), halved lengthwise and sliced into half-moons

2 medium carrots, cut into ½-inch pieces

3 cloves garlic, chopped

½ cup dry white wine

1 (28-ounce) can diced tomatoes, with juice

2 (15-ounce) cans white beans, such as cannellini or Great Northern, rinsed and drained

1 cup loosely packed fresh flat-leaf parsley, chopped

¼ teaspoon kosher salt

¼ teaspoon freshly ground black pepper

2 cups fresh coarse bread crumbs

Preheat the oven to 375°F.

Heat 1 tablespoon of the oil in a large pot over medium-high heat. Add the sausages and cook until browned, 6 to 8 minutes; transfer to a plate and wipe out the pot.

Heat 1 tablespoon of the oil in the same pot over medium-high heat. Add the leeks, carrots, and garlic, and cook, stirring often, until beginning to soften, 5 to 6 minutes.

Add the wine and cook for 1 minute, then add the tomatoes and bring to a boil. Stir in the beans, parsley, salt, and pepper. Transfer to a 3-quart casserole dish.

In a small bowl, combine the bread crumbs with the remaining 1 tablespoon oil. Sprinkle over the bean mixture and bake until the top is golden brown and crispy and the bean mixture is bubbling, about 30 minutes.

COOK'S TIP: To make fresh bread crumbs, place torn pieces of day-old bread into the bowl of a food processor, and pulse a few times until coarse crumbs form. These are great on mac 'n' cheese and other baked casseroles, too.

Red Wine Beef Stew

Prep time: 30 minutes
Total time: 3 hours
Serves 8

Tender and succulent, this red wine–braised beef stew is the ultimate one-pot meal, loaded with tender potatoes and carrots. Don't forget to bring over a loaf of crusty French bread for sopping up the rich sauce. The Butter Lettuce Salad on page 12 is a nice accompaniment.

4 pounds chuck roast, cut into 2-inch pieces

1½ teaspoons kosher salt

1 teaspoon freshly ground black pepper

3 tablespoons all-purpose flour

1 tablespoon olive oil

¼ cup tomato paste

2 cups dry red wine, such as Pinot Noir or Syrah

4 cups low-sodium chicken broth

1 medium yellow onion, quartered

2 bay leaves

4 sprigs thyme

10 medium carrots (about 2 pounds), peeled and cut into 3-inch pieces

1½ pounds baby white or red potatoes, halved

Preheat the oven to 325°F.

Season the meat with salt and pepper, place in a large bowl, and toss with the flour.

Heat the oil in a large Dutch oven or wide-bottomed pot with a tight-fitting lid over medium-high heat. Cook the meat, in batches, until well browned on all sides, 6 to 8 minutes, transferring the pieces to a plate as they are browned. Pour off and discard any drippings from the pot.

Add the tomato paste, wine, broth, onion, bay leaves, thyme, and 2 of the carrots and bring to a boil. Return the meat and any juices back to the pot (the meat should be barely submerged in liquid), cover, and transfer to the oven. Cook for 2 hours.

Using tongs, remove and discard the cooked vegetables. Add the potatoes and the remaining 8 carrots to the pot, cover, and return to the oven. Cook until the meat and vegetables are fork-tender, about 1 hour more.

COOK'S TIP: Stew always tastes better the day after it is made. Let the stew cool to room temperature before refrigerating. Before reheating, skim any visible fat from the surface and cook, covered, over medium-low heat on the stovetop, stirring occasionally, until heated through. Freeze in an airtight container for up to 2 months.

Sweet Potato Torta

Prep time: 20 minutes
Total time: 1 hour 40 minutes
Serves 4 to 6

This creamy, layered vegetarian casserole has—surprise!—no cream. The flaky puff pastry on top makes it downright irresistible. Plus, it's simple to prepare: no precooking involved, only some slicing and grating. We like to serve it with Butter Lettuce Salad (page 12).

1½ pounds russet potatoes (about 3 medium), peeled and sliced into ⅛-inch-thick rounds

10 teaspoons olive oil

1 tablespoon fresh thyme leaves

1½ teaspoons kosher salt

½ teaspoon freshly ground black pepper

½ cup (2 ounces) grated Parmesan cheese

1½ pounds sweet potatoes (about 3), peeled and sliced into ⅛-inch-thick rounds

1 medium beefsteak tomato, sliced into ⅛-inch-thick rounds

1 sheet frozen puff pastry (from a 17.25-ounce package), thawed

Preheat the oven to 375°F. Lightly oil a 9-inch springform pan.

In the bottom of the pan, starting from the outside and working your way in, layer half of the potatoes in concentric circles, overlapping them slightly. Drizzle with 2 teaspoons of the oil and sprinkle with some of the thyme, salt, pepper, and Parmesan. Repeat this process with a layer of half of the sweet potatoes, one layer (all) of the tomato, then with the remaining potatoes and sweet potatoes (don't forget the oil, thyme, salt, pepper, and Parmesan between each layer).

Lay the pastry flat on a work surface and cut into a 9-inch round. Place on top of the vegetables, and, using the tip of a paring knife, cut vents into the pastry. Place the pan on a rimmed baking sheet and bake until the potatoes are tender and easily pierced with a paring knife, about 1 hour 15 minutes. Let rest for 5 minutes before unmolding. Cut into wedges.

COOK'S TIP: Don't be deceived when this torta looks completely cooked at 45 minutes with its browned top; chances are the potatoes aren't quite tender and the puff pastry isn't fully cooked. Be sure to test for doneness with a paring knife, and make sure the pastry is cooked all of the way through.

Roasted Garlic Chicken and Root Vegetables

Prep time: 15 minutes
Total time: 1 hour 15 minutes
Serves 4

Anyone who has received casserole upon casserole will be thrilled when you arrive with a roast chicken. This is a great recipe for doubling: Roast two chickens side by side on one baking sheet, and double the vegetables on a second, placing the vegetables on the lower of the two oven racks to cook.

5 medium carrots (about 1 pound), peeled and cut into 3-inch sticks

1 pound medium parsnips (about 4), peeled and cut into 3-inch sticks

1 head garlic, cloves separated and peeled

12 fresh sage leaves

¼ cup olive oil

1¼ teaspoons kosher salt

½ teaspoon freshly ground black pepper

1 (3½- to 4-pound) chicken

Preheat the oven to 400°F.

On a rimmed baking sheet, toss together the carrots, parsnips, garlic, sage, 3 tablespoons of the oil, ½ teaspoon of the salt, and ¼ teaspoon of the pepper.

Place the chicken on the baking sheet, pushing the vegetables aside as necessary.

Rub the chicken with the remaining 1 tablespoon oil and season with the remaining ¾ teaspoon salt and ¼ teaspoon pepper. Roast, stirring the vegetables once, until the chicken is cooked through, 50 to 60 minutes.

Sweet Pepper and Spinach Lasagne

Prep time: 25 minutes
Total time: 1 hour 20 minutes
Serves 8

This flavorful lasagne—cheesy and veggie-packed, with a hint of sweetness—can serve a large family and then some. No-boil lasagna noodles make it a practical weeknight dinner—so practical that you'll be willing to give one away once in a while.

2 tablespoons olive oil

1 large yellow onion, chopped

2 medium red bell peppers, cored and cut into ½-inch pieces

1 teaspoon kosher salt

2 (10-ounce) packages frozen chopped spinach, thawed

¼ teaspoon freshly ground black pepper

¼ teaspoon crushed red pepper

2 (15-ounce) containers ricotta cheese

2 cups (8 ounces) grated mozzarella cheese

½ cup (2 ounces) grated Parmesan cheese

5 cups Toasted Garlic Marinara (page 65) or store-bought marinara sauce

1 (9-ounce box) no-boil lasagna noodles (16 sheets)

Preheat the oven to 375°F.

Heat the oil in a large skillet over medium-high heat. Add the onion, bell peppers, and ½ teaspoon of the salt and cook, stirring often, until tender, 12 to 15 minutes (decrease the heat, as necessary, to prevent scorching). Squeeze the spinach of any excess water and add to the skillet along with the black pepper, crushed red pepper, and the remaining ½ teaspoon salt; cook, stirring, for 2 minutes.

In a medium bowl, combine the ricotta, 1 cup of the mozzarella, and the Parmesan.

In a 9 by 13-inch baking dish, spread 1 cup of the sauce over the bottom. Top with a layer of 4 lasagna sheets, another 1 cup sauce, one-third of the cheese mixture, and one-third of the vegetable mixture; repeat this layering twice. Top with the remaining lasagna sheets, sauce, and 1 cup mozzarella.

Cover tightly with aluminum foil and bake until the noodles are tender and easily pierced with a knife, 40 to 45 minutes. Remove the foil and continue to bake until the cheese is browned, about 10 minutes. Let rest for 5 minutes before slicing.

COOK'S TIP: Freeze the unbaked lasagne, tightly wrapped with aluminum foil, for up to 2 months. Bake directly from the freezer covered with foil until heated through, about 1 hour.

Roasted Lamb with Parmesan Potatoes and Zucchini

Prep time: 15 minutes
Total time: 55 minutes
Serves 4 to 6

This full meal takes only 15 minutes to put together. Lamb top round is the tenderest piece of the lamb leg and the perfect size roast for 4 to 6 people. Ask your butcher about this prime and well-priced cut.

1½ pounds baby new potatoes, quartered

3 medium zucchini (about 1 pound), halved lengthwise and cut into 1-inch pieces

3 tablespoons olive oil

¼ cup (1 ounce) grated Parmesan cheese

1¾ teaspoons kosher salt

¾ teaspoon freshly ground black pepper

2 pounds lamb top round

1 tablespoon chopped fresh rosemary

1 tablespoon chopped fresh thyme

1 teaspoon grated lemon zest

Preheat the oven to 425°F.

On a rimmed baking sheet, toss together the potatoes, zucchini, 2 tablespoons of the oil, the Parmesan, ¾ teaspoon of the salt, and ¼ teaspoon of the pepper. Roast on the bottom rack, turning once, until golden brown, about 40 minutes.

Meanwhile, season the lamb with the remaining 1 teaspoon salt and ½ teaspoon pepper and place in a small roasting pan. In a small bowl, combine the rosemary, thyme, lemon zest, and the remaining 1 tablespoon oil. Rub evenly over the lamb and roast to the desired doneness, 35 to 40 minutes for medium-rare (internal temperature will be 130°F). Let rest for 5 minutes before slicing.

COOK'S TIP: Resist the urge to turn your potatoes before they release easily from the pan, or else the potatoes' golden brown crust will stick to the pan. Let them roast for a good 30 minutes or so before turning them.

Chorizo, Potato, and Egg Casserole

Prep time: 15 minutes
Total time: 45 minutes
Serves 4 to 6

Spicy Spanish chorizo sausage gives this casserole its sensational smoky flavor. The casserole is versatile, too: perfect for breakfast with toast, for lunch with greens, or for dinner with a loaf of bread and a green salad. Try the Arugula, Radish, Cucumber, and Olive Salad on page 14.

2 tablespoons olive oil

1 large yellow onion, sliced

1 teaspoon kosher salt

1 pound baby red potatoes, thinly sliced

6 to 8 ounces cured Spanish chorizo, thinly sliced

12 large eggs

1 cup (4 ounces) grated Gruyère cheese

1 cup loosely packed fresh flat-leaf parsley, chopped

¼ teaspoon freshly ground black pepper

Preheat the oven to 350°F.

Heat the oil in a large, preferably nonstick, skillet over medium heat. Add the onion and ½ teaspoon of the salt and cook, stirring, until beginning to soften, about 3 minutes. Add the potatoes and cook, covered, stirring occasionally, until the potatoes are tender, 15 to 18 minutes. Add the chorizo and cook for 2 to 3 minutes more. Transfer the mixture to a shallow 2-quart casserole, preferably 8 by 11 inches.

In a large bowl, beat the eggs. Stir in the cheese, parsley, pepper, and the remaining ½ teaspoon salt. Pour over the potato mixture and bake until the center is just set, 25 to 30 minutes.

COOK'S TIP: Look for organic eggs in your grocery store. This ensures that the chicken is fed a hormone- and antibiotic-free diet. Better still, if you can find a local organic source for freshly laid eggs, you'll be hooked.

You can offer comfort and sympathy without turning on your stove.
Here are some simple ways to nourish a grieving family.

• Wine

• Chocolate

• Ice cream and chocolate sauce

• Hot cocoa mix with marshmallows and milk

• Coffee from the local coffee shop

• Tea and honey

• Crackers, cheese, and nuts

• Fresh bagels and cream cheese

• Fresh fruit

Banana-Hazelnut Muffins

Prep time: 20 minutes
Total time: 40 minutes
Makes 12 muffins

This moist, oh-so-scrumptious recipe can easily be made in an 8½-inch loaf pan. If you do this, bake for about 1 hour, until a toothpick inserted into the center comes out clean.

1 cup hazelnuts

2 cups all-purpose flour, spooned and leveled

1½ teaspoons baking powder

¼ teaspoon baking soda

½ teaspoon kosher salt

¼ teaspoon ground cinnamon

Pinch of freshly grated nutmeg

3 ripe bananas

¾ cup sugar

½ cup canola oil

1 large egg

1 teaspoon pure vanilla extract

Preheat the oven to 350°F. Line a regular 12-cup muffin pan with paper liners or spray with nonstick cooking spray.

Spread the hazelnuts on a rimmed baking sheet and bake until toasted and fragrant, 8 to 10 minutes. When cool enough to handle, rub the hazelnuts between a clean kitchen towel to remove the skins (small bits left behind are okay), then coarsely chop.

In a medium bowl, whisk together the flour, baking powder, baking soda, salt, cinnamon, and nutmeg.

In a large bowl, mash the bananas, then whisk in the sugar, oil, egg, and vanilla.

Stir in the flour mixture until just combined (do not overmix). Stir in the hazelnuts.

Divide the batter evenly among the muffin cups and bake until a toothpick inserted into the center of a muffin comes out clean, 18 to 20 minutes. Let cool on a wire rack.

Store the muffins, tightly wrapped, for up to 3 days, or freeze for up to 1 month.

White Chocolate and Macadamia Nut Cookies

Prep time: 20 minutes
Total time: 45 minutes
Makes 40 cookies

These cookies are so decadent and delicious that it's hard to stop at just three.

2 cups all-purpose flour, spooned and leveled

¾ teaspoon baking soda

¾ teaspoon kosher salt

¾ cup (1½ sticks) unsalted butter, at room temperature

¾ cup granulated sugar

¾ cup firmly packed dark brown sugar

1 large egg

1 teaspoon pure vanilla extract

12 ounces white chocolate, chips or chopped

1 cup roasted salted macadamia nuts, coarsely chopped

Preheat the oven to 375°F. Line 2 baking sheets with parchment paper.

In a medium bowl, whisk together the flour, baking soda, and salt.

Working with a stand mixer, preferably fitted with the paddle attachment, or with a hand mixer with a large bowl, beat the butter, granulated sugar, and brown sugar until fluffy, 2 to 3 minutes. Beat in the egg and vanilla. With the mixer on low speed, gradually add the flour mixture and mix until just combined (do not overmix). Stir in the white chocolate and nuts.

Drop heaping tablespoon–size balls of the batter 2 inches apart onto the prepared baking sheets. Bake, rotating the sheets halfway through the baking time, until the edges are golden brown and the centers are just set, 12 to 16 minutes. Let cool for 5 minutes on the baking sheets before transferring the cookies to a wire rack.

COOK'S TIP: Store in an airtight container for up to 3 days.

Brown Sugar Swirl Coffee Cake

Prep time: 15 minutes
Total time: 2 hours (includes cooling time)
Serves 8 to 10

The beauty of a coffee cake is that it's sweet enough for dessert but not too sweet to eat first thing in the morning. Experiment with the swirl in this moist cake by substituting pecans for the walnuts. Raisins or chopped prunes work well as additions, too.

¾ cup walnut halves

⅓ cup dark brown sugar

1 teaspoon ground cinnamon

2 cups all-purpose flour, spooned and leveled

1 teaspoon baking powder

½ teaspoon baking soda

½ teaspoon kosher salt

1 cup (2 sticks) unsalted butter, at room temperature

1 cup granulated sugar

2 large eggs

1 cup sour cream

2 teaspoons pure vanilla extract

Preheat the oven to 350°F. Butter and flour a 12-cup Bundt pan, tapping out the excess flour.

For the swirl, place the walnuts on a baking sheet and bake until toasted and fragrant, 8 to 10 minutes; let cool, then coarsely chop. In a small bowl, combine the walnuts, brown sugar, and cinnamon. Set aside.

In a medium bowl, whisk together the flour, baking powder, baking soda, and salt.

Working with a stand mixer, preferably fitted with the paddle attachment, or with a hand mixer with a large bowl, beat the butter and sugar on medium speed until fluffy, 2 to 3 minutes. Beat in the eggs, one at a time, then the sour cream and vanilla. With the mixer on low speed, gradually mix in the flour mixture until just combined (do not overmix).

Spoon half of the batter evenly into the prepared pan. Sprinkle the swirl mixture over the top of the batter and top with the remaining batter. Bake until a toothpick inserted into the cake comes out with a few moist crumbs attached, 40 to 45 minutes. Let cool for at least 1 hour on a wire rack before inverting onto a plate.

Fresh Apple Cake

Prep time: 20 minutes
Total time: 1 hour
Serves 10

This low-rising cake has a chewy crust and a moist, fresh apple center. Delightful!

3 cups all-purpose flour, spooned and leveled

1½ teaspoons ground cinnamon

1¼ teaspoons baking soda

½ teaspoon kosher salt

3 large eggs

2 cups sugar

1½ teaspoons pure vanilla extract

1 cup (2 sticks) unsalted butter, melted

2 apples, such as Granny Smith or Golden Delicious, peeled, cored, and cut into ½-inch pieces

Sweetened whipped cream, for serving (optional)

Preheat the oven to 350°F. Butter and flour a 9 by 13-inch baking pan, tapping out the excess flour.

In a medium bowl, whisk together the flour, cinnamon, baking soda, and salt.

In a large bowl, whisk together the eggs, sugar, and vanilla, then mix in the butter until well combined. Gradually stir in the flour mixture until just combined (do not overmix); stir in the apples.

Scrape the batter evenly into the prepared pan and bake until a toothpick inserted into the center comes out with a few moist crumbs attached, 35 to 40 minutes. Let cool on a wire rack. Serve with whipped cream, if desired.

||||||||||||||||||||||||||||||||||||||||||||||||||||||||||||||||||||||||||||||||||||||||||||||||

COOK'S TIP: Figure that 1 cup of heavy whipping cream will make about 2 cups of whipped cream. The colder it is, the faster it will whip up. Beat in about 2 tablespoons of confectioners' sugar for every 1 cup cream.

Acknowledgments

We are so grateful to Dana Sullivan for matching us up—great thinking, Dana! Thank you also to our persistent agent, Jane Dystel, and to Jean Lucas at Andrews McMeel for giving us this amazing opportunity.

We are most thankful to our recipe testers for their time, careful attention to detail, and helpful comments. Our testers: Paula Bullwinkel, Deb Cloninger, Allison Cogen, Kathy Conroy, Sara Crosby, Corinne Dedini, Nancy Fleisher, Susan Galecki, Pilar Geisse, Lisa Gilmour, Kirsten Goldstein, Rebecca Gundzik, Grace Hammerstrom, Robin Imagire, Katy Jaeger, Nancy Kruh, Marilyn Lebowitz, Molly McCallum, Elizabeth Melley, Liz Murphy, Sharon Quessenberry, Ann Rosenfield, Ed and Virginia Spencer, Dana Sullivan, Dayna Taus, Tena Watts, and Traci Yerby.

From Sara:

I am thankful to Mom and Gram for inspiring me to cook, to my sister, Tena, for inspiring me to be a good neighbor, and to Michelle for always inspiring me.

Special thanks to Kate Merker for her expert eyes and encouraging words and to Frances Boswell for giving me my start.

From Suzanne:

My husband, Paul, has been exceptionally patient and hardworking as I have cooked my way through this book and, night after night, turned our kitchen into a disaster area. I promise to become a cleaner cook. My boys, Toby and Ian, have introduced me to the joy (!) of cooking with toddlers; you tykes are great helpers and adventurous eaters. Yes, we can make more parsnip soup—if you stop trying to knock each other off the stool.

A big thank-you to the moms who make Central Oregon Families with Multiples such a wonderful group. It was the COFM meal trains that inspired the idea for this book, along with Ann Rosenfield's taco soup, the great meals that Bubbe Evie and Kathy Schindel brought by when the boys were born, and the four days straight that Aunt Shari spent filling our freezer.

To Colleen Dunn Bates and Julie Lowy, many thanks for your insights on helping out recuperating friends. Thanks also to Robin Miller, who helped get this project going.

As always, I am indebted to Nancy Kruh for her brilliant editing.

Metric Conversions and Equivalents

Metric Conversion Formulas

To Convert	Multiply
Ounces to grams	Ounces by 28.35
Pounds to kilograms	Pounds by .454
Teaspoons to milliliters	Teaspoons by 4.93
Tablespoons to milliliters	Tablespoons by 14.79
Fluid ounces to milliliters	Fluid ounces by 29.57
Cups to milliliters	Cups by 236.59
Cups to liters	Cups by .236
Pints to liters	Pints by .473
Quarts to liters	Quarts by .946
Gallons to liters	Gallons by 3.785
Inches to centimeters	Inches by 2.54

Approximate Metric Equivalents

Weight

¼ ounce	7 grams
½ ounce	14 grams
¾ ounce	21 grams
1 ounce	28 grams
1¼ ounces	35 grams
1½ ounces	42.5 grams
1⅔ ounces	45 grams
2 ounces	57 grams
3 ounces	85 grams
4 ounces (¼ pound)	113 grams
5 ounces	142 grams
6 ounces	170 grams
7 ounces	198 grams
8 ounces (½ pound)	227 grams
16 ounces (1 pound)	454 grams
35.25 ounces (2.2 pounds)	1 kilogram

Volume

¼ teaspoon	1 milliliter
½ teaspoon	2.5 milliliters
¾ teaspoon	4 milliliters
1 teaspoon	5 milliliters
1¼ teaspoons	6 milliliters
1½ teaspoons	7.5 milliliters
1¾ teaspoons	8.5 milliliters
2 teaspoons	10 milliliters
1 tablespoon (½ fluid ounce)	15 milliliters
2 tablespoons (1 fluid ounce)	30 milliliters
¼ cup	60 milliliters
⅓ cup	80 milliliters
½ cup (4 fluid ounces)	120 milliliters
⅓ cup	160 milliliters
¾ cup	180 milliliters
1 cup (8 fluid ounces)	240 milliliters
1¼ cups	300 milliliters
1½ cups (12 fluid ounces)	360 milliliters
1⅔ cups	400 milliliters
2 cups (1 pint)	460 milliliters
3 cups	700 milliliters
4 cups (1 quart)	0.95 liter
1 quart plus ¼ cup	1 liter
4 quarts (1 gallon)	3.8 liters

Length

⅛ inch	3 millimeters
¼ inch	6 millimeters
½ inch	1¼ centimeters
1 inch	2½ centimeters
2 inches	5 centimeters
2½ inches	6 centimeters
4 inches	10 centimeters
5 inches	13 centimeters
6 inches	15¼ centimeters
12 inches (1 foot)	30 centimeters

Oven Temperatures

To convert Fahrenheit to Celsius, subtract 32 from Fahrenheit, multiply the result by 5, and then divide by 9.

Description	Fahrenheit	Celsius	British Gas Mark
Very cool	200°	95°	0
Very cool	225°	110°	¼
Very cool	250°	120°	½
Cool	275°	135°	1
Cool	300°	150°	2
Warm	325°	165°	3
Moderate	350°	175°	4
Moderately hot	375°	190°	5
Fairly hot	400°	200°	6
Hot	425°	220°	7
Very hot	450°	230°	8
Very hot	475°	245°	9

Common Ingredients and Their Approximate Equivalents

1 cup uncooked white rice = 185 grams

1 cup all-purpose flour = 140 grams

1 stick butter (4 ounces • ½ cup • 8 tablespoons) = 110 grams

1 cup butter (8 ounces • 2 sticks • 16 tablespoons) = 220 grams

1 cup firmly packed brown sugar = 225 grams

1 cup granulated sugar = 200 grams

Information compiled from a variety of sources, including *Recipes into Type* by Joan Whitman and Dolores Simon (Newton, MA: Biscuit Books, 2000); *The New Food Lover's Companion* by Sharon Tyler Herbst (Hauppauge, NY: Barron's, 1995); and *Rosemary Brown's Big Kitchen Instruction Book* (Kansas City, MO: Andrews McMeel, 1998).

Index

A

Almond-Ginger Bars, 148
almonds, 4, 80, 89, 128, 129, 140, 148
appetizers. *See also* dips
    Bacon-Wrapped Dates, 140
    Caramelized Onion, Bacon, and Blue
        Cheese Tart, 143
    Cold Poached Shrimp with Classic Cocktail
        Sauce, 137
    Lemon and Garlic–Marinated
        Mushrooms, 141
    Parmesan Palmiers, 138
    Rosemary- and Chili-Spiced Cashews, 142
    Sesame Crisps with Hummus, 87
    Slow-Roasted Tomatoes and Garlic with
        Crostini, 145
    Zucchini Relish with Goat Cheese and
        Crackers, 144
appetizers, emergency, 125–29
apple
    Crispy Apple and Chicken Salad with Blue
        Cheese and Basil, 120
    Fresh Apple Cake, 174
    Love Thy Neighbor Apple Pie, 70
    Turkey, Brie, and Apple Baguette, 8
Apricot Crumble Bars, 79
apricot preserves, 79
apricots, 79, 128
arugula, 8, 10, 14, 54, 90, 113, 114, 169
Arugula, Radish, Cucumber, and Olive Salad
    with Balsamic Vinaigrette, 14

Asian
    Asian Chicken Salad Kit, 29
    Asian Noodle Soup, 40
    Cold Sesame Noodle Salad, 121
    Soy-Ginger Chicken Drumsticks, 103
    Thai Watermelon and Shrimp Salad, 96
Asian Chicken Salad Kit, 29
Asian Noodle Soup, 40
avocados, 158
    Chipotle-Pineapple Guacamole, 86

B

baby, newborn, 2–33
baby back ribs, 102
bacon
    Bacon-Wrapped Dates, 140
    Caramelized Onion, Bacon, and Blue
        Cheese Tart, 143
    in salad, 14
Bacon-Wrapped Dates, 140
Balsamic Vinaigrette, 14
banana
    Banana-Hazelnut Muffins, 171
    Peanut Butter, Banana, and Honey
        Smoothie, 6
Banana-Hazelnut Muffins, 171
Barbecue Spiced Chicken with Southwestern
    Slaw, 66
basil, fresh
    Creamy Tomato Baked Ravioli and
        Spinach, 21

Crispy Apple and Chicken Salad with Blue Cheese and Basil, 120
Fresh Ricotta with Soft Herbs, 136
Grilled Zucchini and Eggplant Salad with Basil, 92
Thai Watermelon and Shrimp Salad, 96
bay leaves, 23, 162
beans
Beans and Greens Soup, 41
Burrito Dinner Kit, 28
Hearty Minestrone Soup with Potato Gnocchi, 17
Italian Sausage and White Bean Bake, 161
Red and White Chili, 63
Tuna and Cannellini Bean Salad with Cucumbers and Olives, 119
Beans and Greens Soup, 41
beef
Big-Batch Bolognese, 23
Red Wine Beef Stew, 162
Roast Beef and Cheddar Sandwiches for the Movers, 69
Rosemary Beef with Roasted Tomatoes and Potatoes, 50
bell pepper, 20, 29, 63, 68, 123, 144, 166
berries
Blueberry-Blackberry Cobbler, 108
Brown Butter Blueberry Muffins, 33
Chewy Raspberry-Walnut Meringues, 146
cranberries, 4, 160
Fresh Fruit and Yogurt Cups, 5
Fresh Raspberry–Ricotta Tart, 116
Mixed Berry and Banana Smoothie, 6
Raspberry-Peach Smoothie, 7
Raspberry-Rhubarb Crumble Pie, 72
Big-Batch Bolognese, 23
black beans, 28
block parties and barbecues, 85–109
blue cheese
Crispy Apple and Chicken Salad with Blue Cheese and Basil, 120
Onion, Bacon, and Blue Cheese Tart, 143
Platter of Tomatoes with Pepperoncini Vinaigrette, 95

blueberries
Blueberry-Blackberry Cobbler, 108
Brown Butter Blueberry Muffins, 33
Blueberry-Blackberry Cobbler, 108
bocconcini, 94
book clubs, 133–51
bread crumbs, homemade, 161
breads
Cheddar-Scallion Cornbread, 64
Really Good Biscuits, 9
Tomato and Oregano Flatbread, 122
breads, sweet
Banana-Hazelnut Muffins, 171
Brown Butter Blueberry Muffins, 33
Golden Raisin–Rosemary Scones, 117
Oat-Nut Scones, 55
Spiced Pumpkin–Walnut Bread, 127
Zucchini-Orange Bread, 56
breakfast
Brown Butter Blueberry Muffins, 33
Brown Sugar Swirl Coffee Cake, 173
Chorizo, Potato, and Egg Casserole, 169
Fresh Raspberry–Ricotta Tart, 116
Golden Raisin–Rosemary Scones, 117
Gruyère and Arugula Scrambled Egg Roll-Ups, 114
Oat-Nut Scones, 55
Sliced Egg, Radish, Caper Baguettes, 115
Brie cheese, 8
Brown Butter Blueberry Muffins, 33
Brown Sugar Swirl Coffee Cake, 173
bulgur wheat, 42
Burrito Dinner Kit, 28
Butter Lettuce Salad with Toasted Pine Nuts, Herbs, and Citrus Vinaigrette, 12
buttermilk, 55, 64, 106
Butternut Squash and Farro Soup, 157

C

cabbage, 17, 66, 124
Caesar-Like Salad with Croutons, 15
Caesar-Like Vinaigrette, 16

cakes
Brown Sugar Swirl Coffee Cake, 173
Chocolate Pecan Sheet Cake, 105
Fresh Apple Cake, 174
moistness, 107
Olive Oil and Cornmeal Cake, 126
Right-Side-Up Peach Cake, 106
sheet cake storage, 105
Sweet Tangerine Cake, 150
candied ginger, 32, 149
cannellini beans, 41, 63, 161
cantaloupe, 94
Caramelized Onion, Bacon, and Blue Cheese
Tart, 143
Caraway Cabbage Slaw, 124
cashews, 29, 142
cauliflower, Roasted Cauliflower Macaroni
and Cheese, 46
cayenne pepper, 63, 89, 102, 156
Cheddar cheese, 64, 69, 124
Cheddar-Scallion Cornbread, 64
cheese
blue, 95, 120, 143
Brie, 8
Cheddar, 64, 69, 124
cheese platter, 139
Feta, 11, 88, 93
Gruyère, 26, 114, 118
Jack, 28, 101
Manchego, 135
mozzarella, 26, 94, 97, 166
Parmesan, 17, 21, 26, 41, 45, 54, 89, 98,
138, 140, 164, 166, 168
ravioli, 21
ricotta, 116, 136
Chewy Gingersnaps, 32
Chewy Raspberry-Walnut Meringues, 146
chicken
Asian Chicken Salad Kit, 29
Barbecue Spiced Chicken with
Southwestern Slaw, 66
Chicken and Vegetable Soup with Lemon,
38
Chicken Cacciatore with Mashed
Potatoes, 48

Chicken Tortilla Soup, 158
Chicken Two Ways, 28–29
Crispy Apple and Chicken Salad with Blue
Cheese and Basil, 120
grocery deli, 68
Lemon-Thyme Chicken Skewers, 104
Pepper Jack Chicken Enchiladas with
Tomatillo Sauce, 100–101
Roasted Garlic Chicken and Root
Vegetables, 165
Savory Chicken Cobbler, 68
Soy-Ginger Chicken Drumsticks, 103
Spring Vegetable Chicken Potpie, 24–25
Stewed Chicken with Chickpeas and
Lemon, 52
Chicken and Vegetable Soup with Lemon, 38
chicken broth, 17, 18, 24, 39, 41, 68, 100,
156, 157, 158, 162
Chicken Cacciatore with Mashed Potatoes, 48
Chicken Tortilla Soup, 158
Chicken Two Ways, 28–29
Chickpea and Cucumber Tabbouleh, 42
chickpeas
Chickpea and Cucumber Tabbouleh, 42
Chopped Chickpea, Parsley, and Pepper
Salad Sandwich, 123
Sesame Crisps with Hummus, 87
Stewed Chicken with Chickpeas and
Lemon, 52
chili, Red and White Chili, 63
chili powder, 63, 142, 160
chili-garlic sauce, 121
Chili-Rubbed Roast Turkey Breast and
Jalapeño Cranberry Sandwiches, 160
Chinese noodles, 40
Chipotle-Pineapple Guacamole, 86
chipotles, 15, 86, 98, 102
chocolate
Chocolate Chip and Candied Ginger
Blondies, 149
Chocolate Pecan Sheet Cake, 105
Chocolate Pudding Pots, 30
Coconut-Almond Haystacks, 128
Crunchy Milk Chocolate Oatmeal Bars, 129
Extra-Fudgy Brownies, 74

Peanut Butter Chip Chocolate Cookies, 109
Roasted Almond–Chocolate Chip Cookies, 80
White Chocolate and Macadamia Nut
    Cookies, 172
Chocolate Chip and Candied Ginger
    Blondies, 149
chocolate chips, 128, 149, 172
Chocolate Pecan Sheet Cake, 105
Chocolate Pudding Pots, 30
Chopped Chickpea, Parsley, and Pepper
    Salad Sandwich, 123
Chorizo, Potato, and Egg Casserole, 169
cilantro, 29, 66, 93, 100, 121, 156, 158
Citrus Vinaigrette, 13
coconut, 128
Coconut-Almond Haystacks, 128
Cold Poached Shrimp with Classic Cocktail
    Sauce, 137
Cold Sesame Noodle Salad, 121
condolences, 155–74
cookies
    Almond-Ginger Bars, 148
    Apricot Crumble Bars, 79
    Chewy Gingersnaps, 32
    Chocolate Chip and Candied Ginger
        Blondies, 149
    Coconut-Almond Haystacks, 128
    Cranberry Granola Bars, 4
    Crunchy Milk Chocolate Oatmeal Bars, 129
    Earl Grey Shortbread Cookies, 147
    Lemon-Glazed Pistachio Shortbread
        Cookies, 76
    Peanut Butter Chip Chocolate Cookies, 109
    Peanut Crunch Cookies, 57
    Roasted Almond–Chocolate Chip Cookies, 80
    White Chocolate and Macadamia Nut
        Cookies, 172
Cook's Tips
    adding parsley, 141
    almonds, 89
    apricot cookies, 79
    avocados, 86
    bacon in salad, 14
    biscuit dough, 9
    cake moistness, 107

canned tuna, 119
Caramelized Onion, Bacon, and Blue
    Cheese Tart, 143
casserole assembly and delivery, 21
chicken preparation, 120
chocolate, 74
choosing and storing corn, 93
cobbler, 108
cookie glaze, 76
cookie storage, 109, 172
cookie yield, 147
crabmeat, 134
crumble pie dough, 73
delivering stew and grains, 53
egg whites, 146
enchiladas, 101
flakey and tender scones, 55
freezing for later use, 17, 33, 45, 56, 81,
    138, 156
French lentils de Puy, 22
go-to-meal for one or two people, 47
grilled chicken, 103
grocery deli chicken, 29
hard-boiled eggs, 115
homemade bread crumbs, 161
hummus, 87
lasagne in advance, 27, 167
macaroni and cheese, 161
marinade, 121
nectarines in salad, 14
organic eggs, 169
parchment packets, 51
parsley butter, 98
pasilla chilies, 159
peeling butternut squash, 157
pickle ratio, 62
pie dough, 71
pizza dough, 122
pork or beef, 23
pot pie filling, 25
prosciutto, 94
red wine vinegar, 14
reheating mashed potatoes, 49
rice, 18
ricotta, 136

Cooks tips (continued)
  roast potatoes, 168
  salad seasoning, 91
  salami, 97
  scone storage, 117
  sheet cake storage, 105
  shrimp and cocktail sauce, 137
  shrimp salad, 96
  smoothie packets, 7
  spinach, 118
  stews, 163
  tomatoes, 95, 145
  torta baking time, 164
  turkey chili, 63
  walnuts in salad, 14
  whipped cream, 174
corn, 68, 93, 98, 101, 156
couscous, 52
cranberries, 4, 160
Cranberry Granola Bars, 4
cream, heavy, 21, 68, 100, 105, 108, 117, 148, 174
Creamy Tomato Baked Ravioli and Spinach, 21
crème fraîche, 126
Crispy Apple and Chicken Salad with Blue
  Cheese and Basil, 120
Crunchy Milk Chocolate Oatmeal Bars, 129
crushed red pepper, 23, 26, 62, 92, 166
crust, pie, 70
Crustless Spinach Quiche, 118
cucumber, 14, 20, 29, 42, 62, 121
  Cucumber, Celery, Sprout, and Cream
    Cheese Sandwich, 8
  Cucumber, Feta, and Dill Salsa, 88
  Cucumber and Potato Salad with
    Mustard-Dill Vinaigrette, 91
  Tuna and Cannellini Bean Salad with
    Cucumbers and Olives, 119

Blueberry-Blackberry Cobbler, 108
Brown Sugar Swirl Coffee Cake, 173
cake moistness, 107
Chewy Gingersnaps, 32
Chewy Raspberry-Walnut Meringues, 146
Chocolate Chip and Candied Ginger
  Blondies, 149
Chocolate Pecan Sheet Cake, 105
Chocolate Pudding Pots, 30
Coconut-Almond Haystacks, 128
Cranberry Granola Bars, 4
Crunchy Milk Chocolate Oatmeal Bars, 129
Earl Grey Shortbread Cookies, 147
Extra-Fudgy Brownies, 74
Fresh Apple Cake, 174
Fresh Raspberry–Ricotta Tart, 116
Lemon-Glazed Pistachio Shortbread
  Cookies, 76
Love Thy Neighbor Apple Pie, 70
Nectarine Crisp, 31
Olive Oil and Cornmeal Cake, 126
Right-Side-Up Peach Cake, 106
sheet cake storage, 105
Sweet Tangerine Cake, 150
White Chocolate and Macadamia Nut
  Cookies, 172
dill, 11, 62, 91
dill, fresh, 45, 88
dips
  Chipotle-Pineapple Guacamole, 86
  Cucumber, Feta, and Dill Salsa, 88
  Fresh Ricotta with Soft Herbs, 136
  Lime and Chile Crab Dip, 134
  Roasted Red Pepper Dip, 89
  Smashed Peas with Manchego and
    Lemon, 135
drumsticks, 103

D

dates, 140
desserts
  Almond-Ginger Bars, 148
  Apricot Crumble Bars, 79

E

Earl Grey Shortbread Cookies, 147
Easy-Bake Eggplant Lasagne, 26–27
egg dishes
  Chorizo, Potato, and Egg Casserole, 169

Crustless Spinach Quiche, 118
Gruyère and Arugula Scrambled Egg
Roll-Ups, 114
Sliced Egg, Radish, Caper Baguettes, 115
Zucchini and Parmesan Frittata, 54
eggplant, 26–27, 92
enchiladas, 100–101
espresso powder, 102
Extra-Fudgy Brownies, 74

F

fennel bulb, 10
Feta cheese, 11, 88, 93
finger foods
Bacon-Wrapped Dates, 140
Caramelized Onion, Bacon, and Blue
Cheese Tart, 143
Chili-Rubbed Roast Turkey Breast and
Jalapeño Cranberry Sandwich, 160
Chopped Chickpea, Parsley, and Pepper
Salad Sandwich, 123
Cold Poached Shrimp with Classic Cocktail
Sauce, 137
Crunchy Milk Chocolate Oatmeal Bars, 129
Crustless Spinach Quiche, 118
Cucumber, Celery, Sprout, and Cream
Cheese Sandwich, 8
Golden Raisin–Rosemary Scones, 117
Gruyère and Arugula Scrambled Egg
Roll-Ups, 114
Ham Sandwich with Caraway Cabbage
Slaw and Pickles, 124
Lemon and Garlic–Marinated
Mushrooms, 141
Parmesan Palmiers, 138
Roast Beef and Cheddar Sandwiches for
the Movers, 69
Rosemary- and Chili-Spiced Cashews, 142
Slow-Roasted Tomatoes and Garlic with
Crostini, 145
Spiced Pumpkin–Walnut Bread, 127
Tomato and Oregano Flatbread, 122
Turkey, Brie, and Apple Baguette, 8

Turkey Sandwich with Cheddar, Tomato,
Sprouts, and Smoked Paprika
Mayonnaise, 124
Zucchini Relish with Goat Cheese and
Crackers, 144
fish/seafood
Cold Poached Shrimp with Classic Cocktail
Sauce, 137
Halibut, Leek, and Carrot Parchment
Packets, 51
Lime and Chile Crab Dip, 134
Thai Watermelon and Shrimp Salad, 96
Tuna and Cannellini Bean Salad with
Cucumbers and Olives, 119
French lentils de Puy, 22
Fresh Apple Cake, 174
Fresh Fruit and Yogurt Cups, 5
Fresh Raspberry–Ricotta Tart, 116
Fresh Ricotta with Soft Herbs, 136

G

ginger
candied, 32, 149
fresh, 39, 72, 96, 103, 121, 148
goat cheese, 144
Golden Raisin–Rosemary Scones, 117
grains
bulgur wheat, 42
couscous, 52
farro, 157
quinoa, 43
rice, long-grain white, 18
Great Northern beans, 161
green bell pepper, 63
green lentils, 22
Grilled Corn on the Cob with Chipotle and
Parsley Butters, 98
Grilled Zucchini and Eggplant Salad with
Basil, 92
Gruyère and Arugula Scrambled Egg
Roll-Ups, 114
Gruyère cheese, 26, 114, 118, 169

H

Halibut, Leek, and Carrot Parchment Packets, 51

Ham Sandwich with Caraway Cabbage Slaw and Pickles, 124

hazelnuts, 171

Hearty Minestrone Soup with Potato Gnocchi, 17

honey, 5, 6, 160

horseradish, 137

hummus, 87

I

Italian
   Big-Batch Bolognese, 23
   Chicken Cacciatore with Mashed Potatoes, 48
   Creamy Tomato Baked Ravioli and Spinach, 21
   Easy-Bake Eggplant Lasagne, 26–27
   Hearty Minestrone Soup with Potato Gnocchi, 17
   Italian Sausage and White Bean Bake, 161
   Prosciutto and Melon with Mozzarella and Mint, 94
   Romaine Salad with Salami, Mozzarella, and Peppadew Peppers, 97
   Spaghetti Kit: Toasted Garlic Marinara, Pasta, and Fresh Bread, 65
   Sweet Pepper and Spinach Lasagne, 166
   Zucchini and Parmesan Frittata, 54
Italian sausage, 22, 161
Italian Sausage and White Bean Bake, 161

J

Jack cheese, 28, 101

jalapeño chilies, 93, 100, 134

Jar of Quick Garlic-Dill Pickles, 62

K

kale, 41

kidney beans, 17, 63

L

lamb, Roasted Lamb with Parmesan Potatoes and Zucchini, 168

lasagne
   Easy-Bake Eggplant Lasagne, 26–27
   Sweet Pepper and Spinach Lasagne, 166
leeks, 24, 51, 161
lemon
   Chicken and Vegetable Soup with Lemon, 38
   Lemon and Garlic–Marinated Mushrooms, 141
   Lemon-Glazed Pistachio Shortbread Cookies, 76
   Lemon-Thyme Chicken Skewers, 104
   Lemony Potato and Fennel Salad with Arugula, 10
   Smashed Peas with Manchego and Lemon, 135
   Stewed Chicken with Chickpeas and Lemon, 52
Lemon and Garlic–Marinated Mushrooms, 141
lemon juice, 10, 38, 43, 70, 76, 87, 88, 95, 120, 135, 137
lemon zest, 32, 52, 76, 104, 116, 168
Lemon-Glazed Pistachio Shortbread Cookies, 76
Lemon-Thyme Chicken Skewers, 104
Lemony Potato and Fennel Salad with Arugula, 10
lettuce, 29, 69, 97
Lime and Chile Crab Dip, 134
lime juice, 66, 86, 93, 96, 98, 134, 158
lime zest, 134
Love Thy Neighbor Apple Pie, 70

M

macadamia nuts, 172
macaroni and cheese, 46, 161
main dishes
  Barbecue Spiced Chicken with
    Southwestern Slaw, 66
  Big-Batch Bolognese, 23
  Chicken Cacciatore with Mashed
    Potatoes, 48
  Chicken Two Ways, 28–29
  Chili-Rubbed Roast Turkey Breast and
    Jalapeño Cranberry Sandwiches, 160
  Chorizo, Potato, and Egg Casserole, 169
  Creamy Tomato Baked Ravioli and
    Spinach, 21
  Easy-Bake Eggplant Lasagne, 26–27
  Halibut, Leek, and Carrot Parchment
    Packets, 51
  Italian Sausage and White Bean Bake, 161
  Lemon-Thyme Chicken Skewers, 104
  Pepper Jack Chicken Enchiladas with
    Tomatillo Sauce, 100–101
  Red and White Chili, 63
  Red Wine Beef Stew, 162
  Roasted Cauliflower Macaroni and
    Cheese, 46
  Roasted Garlic Chicken and Root
    Vegetables, 165
  Roasted Lamb with Parmesan Potatoes
    and Zucchini, 168
  Rosemary Beef with Roasted Tomatoes
    and Potatoes, 50
  Sausage and Lentil Stew, 22
  Savory Chicken Cobbler, 68
  Soy-Ginger Chicken Drumsticks, 103
  Spiced Coffee–Rubbed Baby Back Ribs, 102
  Spring Vegetable Chicken Potpie, 24–25
  Stewed Chicken with Chickpeas and
    Lemon, 52
  Sweet Pepper and Spinach Lasagne, 166
  Sweet Potato Torta, 164
  Turkey and Dill Meatloaf, 45
  Zucchini and Parmesan Frittata, 54

Manchego cheese, 135
maple syrup, 4
meat, 97, 140
  Ham Sandwich with Caraway Cabbage
    Slaw and Pickles, 124
  Italian Sausage and White Bean Bake, 161
  Prosciutto and Melon with Mozzarella
    and Mint, 94
  Red Wine Beef Stew, 162
  Roast Beef and Cheddar Sandwiches for
    the Movers, 69
  Roasted Lamb with Parmesan Potatoes
    and Zucchini, 168
  Rosemary Beef with Roasted Tomatoes
    and Potatoes, 50
  Spiced Coffee–Rubbed Baby Back Ribs, 102
  Turkey and Dill Meatloaf, 45
meatloaf, 45
Mediterranean
  Chickpea and Cucumber Tabbouleh, 42
  Lemon-Thyme Chicken Skewers, 104
  Stewed Chicken with Chickpeas and
    Lemon, 52
  Tomato and Oregano Flatbread, 122
  Tuna and Cannellini Bean Salad with
    Cucumbers and Olives, 119
meetings and gatherings, 112–24
melon
  Prosciutto and Melon with Mozzarella
    and Mint, 94
  Thai Watermelon and Shrimp Salad, 96
metric conversion formulas, 178
metric weight equivalents, 178
Mexican
  Burrito Dinner Kit, 28
  Chicken Tortilla Soup, 158
  Chipotle-Pineapple Guacamole, 86
  Chorizo, Potato, and Egg Casserole, 169
  Lime and Chile Crab Dip, 134
  Pepper Jack Chicken Enchiladas with
    Tomatillo Sauce, 100–101
  Summer Gazpacho, 20
mint, fresh, 42, 94, 96
Mixed Berry and Banana Smoothie, 6

molasses, 32

mozzarella cheese, 26, 94, 97, 166

muffins

    Banana-Hazelnut Muffins, 171

    Brown Butter Blueberry Muffins, 33

mushrooms, 40, 48, 141

Mustard-Dill Vinaigrette, 91

N

napa cabbage, 124

Nectarine Crisp, 31

neighborhood, welcome to, 61–81

nuts

    Apricot Crumble Bars, 79

    Banana-Hazelnut Muffins, 171

    Brown Sugar Swirl Coffee Cake, 173

    Butter Lettuce Salad with Toasted Pine
        Nuts, Herbs, and Citrus Vinaigrette, 12

    Cold Sesame Noodle Salad, 121

    Lemon-Glazed Pistachio Shortbread
        Cookies, 76

    Oat-Nut Scones, 55

    Peanut Crunch Cookies, 57

    Roasted Almond–Chocolate Chip Cookies,
        80

    Roasted Red Pepper Dip, 89

    Rosemary- and Chili-Spiced Cashews, 142

    White Chocolate and Macadamia Nut
        Cookies, 172

O

Oat-Nut Scones, 55

oats

    Apricot Crumble Bars, 79

    Cranberry Granola Bars, 4

    Crunchy Milk Chocolate Oatmeal Bars, 129

    Nectarine Crisp, 31

    Oat-Nut Scones, 55

Olive Oil and Cornmeal Cake, 126

orange juice, 160

orange zest, 56

Orzo Salad with Tomatoes, Feta, and Dill, 11

P

Parmesan cheese, 17, 21, 26, 41, 45, 54, 89,
    98, 138, 140, 164, 166, 168

Parmesan Palmiers, 138

parsnip, 39, 165

pasilla chilies, 158

peaches, 7, 106

peanut butter

    Peanut Butter, Banana, and Honey
        Smoothie, 6

    Peanut Butter Chip Chocolate Cookies, 109

    Peanut Crunch Cookies, 57

    Peanut Butter, Banana, and Honey
        Smoothie, 6

Peanut Butter Chip Chocolate Cookies, 109

peanut butter chips, 109

Peanut Crunch Cookies, 57

peanuts, 57, 121

peas, 24, 135

pecans, 79

peppadew peppers, 97

Pepper Jack Chicken Enchiladas with
    Tomatillo Sauce, 100–101

pepperoncini, 95

pickles, 62, 124

pineapple, 86

pineapple juice, 7

Pinot Noir, 162

pinto beans, 28

pistachios, 76

Platter of Tomatoes with Pepperoncini
    Vinaigrette, 95

pork

    Big-Batch Bolognese, 23

    Ham Sandwich with Caraway Cabbage
        Slaw and Pickles, 124

    Spiced Coffee–Rubbed Baby Back Ribs, 102

potato

    Chicken Cacciatore with Mashed
        Potatoes, 48

    Chorizo, Potato, and Egg Casserole, 169

    Cucumber and Potato Salad with
        Mustard-Dill Vinaigrette, 91

Hearty Minestrone Soup with Potato Gnocchi, 17

Lemony Potato and Fennel Salad with Arugula, 10

Red Wine Beef Stew, 162

Roasted Lamb with Parmesan Potatoes and Zucchini, 168

Rosemary Beef with Roasted Tomatoes and Potatoes, 50

Smoky Corn Chowder, 156

Sweet Potato Torta, 164

Prosciutto and Melon with Mozzarella and Mint, 94

pudding, Chocolate Pudding Pots, 30

puff pastry, frozen, 24, 138, 143, 164

pumpkin puree, 127

Q

quinoa, 43

Quinoa-Walnut-Celery Salad, 43

R

radish, 115, 136

raisins, 66, 117

raspberries, 72, 116

raspberry jam, 146

raspberry sorbet, 7

Raspberry-Peach Smoothie, 7

Raspberry-Rhubarb Crumble Pie, 72

Really Good Biscuits, 9

Red and White Chili, 63

red bell pepper, 20, 29, 68, 123, 166

Red Wine Beef Stew, 162

rhubarb, 72

rice, long-grain white, 18

rice vinegar, 29

ricotta, 116, 136

Right-Side-Up Peach Cake, 106

Roast Beef and Cheddar Sandwiches for the Movers, 69

Roasted Almond–Chocolate Chip Cookies, 80

Roasted Cauliflower Macaroni and Cheese, 46

Roasted Garlic Chicken and Root Vegetables, 165

Roasted Lamb with Parmesan Potatoes and Zucchini, 168

Roasted Red Pepper Dip, 89

Romaine Salad with Salami, Mozzarella, and Peppadew Peppers, 97

rosemary, fresh, 41, 48, 50, 117, 142, 168

Rosemary Beef with Roasted Tomatoes and Potatoes, 50

Rosemary- and Chili-Spiced Cashews, 142

S

sage leaves, 165

salad dressings

Balsamic Vinaigrette, 14

Caesar-Like Vinaigrette, 16

Citrus Vinaigrette, 13

Mustard-Dill Vinaigrette, 91

Pepperoncini Vinaigrette, 95

salads

Arugula, Radish, Cucumber, and Olive Salad with Balsamic Vinaigrette, 14

Balsamic Vinaigrette, 14

Butter Lettuce Salad with Toasted Pine Nuts, Herbs, and Citrus Vinaigrette, 12

Caesar-Like Salad with Croutons, 15

Caesar-Like Vinaigrette, 16

Caraway Cabbage Slaw, 124

Citrus Vinaigrette, 13

Cold Sesame Noodle Salad, 121

Crispy Apple and Chicken Salad with Blue Cheese and Basil, 120

Cucumber and Potato Salad with Mustard-Dill Vinaigrette, 91

Grilled Zucchini and Eggplant Salad with Basil, 92

Platter of Tomatoes with Pepperoncini Vinaigrette, 95

Romaine Salad with Salami, Mozzarella, and Peppadew Peppers, 97

Southwestern Slaw, 66

Salads (continued)
    Summer Corn Salad with Chiles, Lime,
        and Feta, 93
    Thai Watermelon and Shrimp Salad, 96
salami, 97
sandwiches
    Chili-Rubbed Roast Turkey Breast and
        Jalapeño Cranberry Sandwiches, 160
    Chopped Chickpea, Parsley, and Pepper
        Salad Sandwich, 123
    Cucumber, Celery, Sprout, and Cream
        Cheese Sandwich, 8
    Ham Sandwich with Caraway Cabbage
        Slaw and Pickles, 124
    Roast Beef and Cheddar Sandwiches for
        the Movers, 69
    Turkey, Brie, and Apple Baguette, 8
    Turkey Sandwich with Cheddar, Tomato,
        Sprouts, and Smoked Paprika
        Mayonnaise, 124
Sausage and Lentil Stew, 22
Savory Chicken Cobbler, 68
scallion, 29, 40, 43, 64, 66, 91, 96, 120, 121,
    123, 134
Sesame Crisps with Hummus, 87
sesame oil, 40, 121
sesame seeds, 87
shortbread cookies, 147
shrimp
    Cold Poached Shrimp with Classic Cocktail
        Sauce, 137
    Thai Watermelon and Shrimp Salad, 96
sickness, recovery of, 36–57
Sliced Egg, Radish, Caper Baguettes, 115
Slow-Roasted Tomatoes and Garlic with
    Crostini, 145
Smashed Peas with Manchego and Lemon, 135
smoked paprika, 124, 156
Smoky Corn Chowder, 156
smoothies
    Mixed Berry and Banana Smoothie, 6
    Peanut Butter, Banana, and Honey
        Smoothie, 6
    Raspberry-Peach Smoothie, 7

snacks
    Banana-Hazelnut Muffins, 171
    Brown Butter Blueberry Muffins, 33
    Cranberry Granola Bars, 4
    Fresh Fruit and Yogurt Cups, 5
    Golden Raisin–Rosemary Scones, 117
    Oat-Nut Scones, 55
    Orzo Salad with Tomatoes, Feta, and Dill, 11
    Really Good Biscuits, 9
    Spiced Pumpkin–Walnut Bread, 127
    Three Smoothie Kits, 6–7
    Two Surprise Sandwiches, 8
    Zucchini and Parmesan Frittata, 54
    Zucchini-Orange Bread, 56
soups
    Asian Noodle Soup, 40
    Beans and Greens Soup, 41
    Big-Batch Bolognese, 23
    Butternut Squash and Farro Soup, 157
    Chicken and Vegetable Soup with Lemon,
        38
    Chicken Tortilla Soup, 158
    Hearty Minestrone Soup with Potato
        Gnocchi, 17
    Red Wine Beef Stew, 162
    Sausage and Lentil Stew, 22
    Smoky Corn Chowder, 156
    Summer Tomato Gazpacho, 20
    Sweet Potato, Parsnip, and Ginger Soup, 39
    Sweet Potato and Rice Soup, 18
Soy-Ginger Chicken Drumsticks, 103
Spaghetti Kit: Toasted Garlic Marinara,
    Pasta, and Fresh Bread, 65
Spanish chorizo, 169
Spiced Coffee–Rubbed Baby Back Ribs, 102
Spiced Pumpkin–Walnut Bread, 127
spinach, 118, 166
Spring Vegetable Chicken Potpie, 24–25
sprouts, 8, 124
Stewed Chicken with Chickpeas and Lemon, 52
sumac, 87
Summer Corn Salad with Chiles, Lime, and
    Feta, 93
Summer Tomato Gazpacho, 20

sweet breads. *See also* cakes
  Banana-Hazelnut Muffins, 171
  Brown Butter Blueberry Muffins, 33
  Golden Raisin–Rosemary Scones, 117
  Oat-Nut Scones, 55
  Spiced Pumpkin–Walnut Bread, 127
  Zucchini-Orange Bread, 56
Sweet Pepper and Spinach Lasagne, 166
sweet potato, 18, 39, 164
Sweet Potato, Parsnip, and Ginger Soup, 39
Sweet Potato Torta, 164
Sweet Tangerine Cake, 150
Swiss chard, 22
sympathy without cooking, 170
Syrah, 162

T

tangerine zest/juice, 150
tarragon, 134, 136
tea leaves, 147
Thai Watermelon and Shrimp Salad, 96
Three Green Salads and Three Vinaigrettes,
  12–16
thyme leaves, 18, 22, 68, 144, 145, 162, 164, 168
  Lemon-Thyme Chicken Skewers, 104
Toasted Garlic Marinara, 65
Tomatillo Sauce, 100
tomatillos, 100
tomato
  canned, 26, 63, 157, 161
  fresh, 8, 11, 17, 20, 22, 48, 69, 158
  paste, 23, 63, 162
  Platter of Tomatoes with Pepperoncini
    Vinaigrette, 95
  Rosemary Beef with Roasted Tomatoes
    and Potatoes, 50
  Slow-Roasted Tomatoes and Garlic with
    Crostini, 145
  Sweet Potato Torta, 164
  Toasted Garlic Marinara, 65
  Tomato and Oregano Flatbread, 122
  Turkey Sandwich with Cheddar, Tomato,
    Sprouts, and Smoked Paprika
    Mayonnaise, 124

Tomato and Oregano Flatbread, 122
Tuna and Cannellini Bean Salad with
  Cucumbers and Olives, 119
turkey, 8, 45, 124, 160
Turkey, Brie, and Apple Baguette, 8
Turkey and Dill Meatloaf, 45
Turkey Sandwich with Cheddar, Tomato,
  Sprouts, and Smoked Paprika
  Mayonnaise, 124

V

vegetarian
  Chickpea and Cucumber Tabbouleh, 42
  Chipotle-Pineapple Guacamole, 86
  Chopped Chickpea, Parsley, and Pepper
    Salad Sandwich, 123
  Cold Sesame Noodle Salad, 121
  Creamy Tomato Baked Ravioli and
    Spinach, 21
  Crustless Spinach Quiche, 118
  Cucumber, Feta, and Dill Salsa, 88
  Cucumber and Potato Salad with
    Mustard-Dill Vinaigrette, 91
  Easy-Bake Eggplant Lasagne, 26–27
  Fresh Ricotta with Soft Herbs, 136
  Grilled Corn on the Cob with Chipotle
    and Parsley Butters, 98
  Grilled Zucchini and Eggplant Salad with
    Basil, 92
  Gruyère and Arugula Scrambled Egg
    Roll-Ups, 114
  Jar of Quick Garlic-Dill Pickles, 62
  Lemon and Garlic–Marinated
    Mushrooms, 141
  Lemony Potato and Fennel Salad with
    Arugula, 10
  Orzo Salad with Tomatoes, Feta, and Dill, 11
  Parmesan Palmiers, 138
  Platter of Tomatoes with Pepperoncini
    Vinaigrette, 95
  Quinoa-Walnut-Celery Salad, 43
  Roasted Cauliflower Macaroni and
    Cheese, 46
  Roasted Red Pepper Dip, 89

Vegetarian (*continued*)
   Rosemary- and Chili-Spiced Cashews, 142
   Sesame Crisps with Hummus, 87
   Sliced Egg, Radish, Caper Baguettes, 115
   Slow-Roasted Tomatoes and Garlic with
      Crostini, 145
   Smashed Peas with Manchego and
      Lemon, 135
   Spaghetti Kit: Toasted Garlic Marinara,
      Pasta, and Fresh Bread, 65
   Summer Corn Salad with Chiles, Lime,
      and Feta, 93
   Summer Tomato Gazpacho, 20
   Sweet Pepper and Spinach Lasagne, 166
   Sweet Potato Torta, 164
   Three Green Salads and Three
      Vinaigrettes, 12–16
   Tomato and Oregano Flatbread, 122
   Zucchini and Parmesan Frittata, 54
   Zucchini Relish with Goat Cheese and
      Crackers, 144
volume equivalents, 179

W
watermelon, 96
welcome, to neighborhood, 61–81
White Chocolate and Macadamia Nut
   Cookies, 172

Y
yellow bell peppers, 144
yogurt, 5, 6, 7

Z
zucchini, 45, 54, 56, 101, 144
   Grilled Zucchini and Eggplant Salad with
      Basil, 92
   Roasted Lamb with Parmesan Potatoes
      and Zucchini, 168
Zucchini and Parmesan Frittata, 54
Zucchini Relish with Goat Cheese and
   Crackers, 144
Zucchini-Orange Bread, 56

About the Authors

Sara Quessenberry is the recipe developer and food stylist for *Real Simple magazine*. With her easy-to-follow, time-saving recipes and down-to-earth approach, Quessenberry makes cooking seem like an inviting opportunity rather than a daunting task. She resides in New York City.

Suzanne Schlosberg is a health, nutrition, and parenting writer known for her humorous, accessible approach to lifestyl topics.. A former senior editor of *Shape* magazine, she is the author or coauthor of ten books, including *Fitness for Dummies*, *The Ultimate Diet Log*, and *The Essential Breastfeeding Log*. Her articles have appeared in *Ladies' Home Journal*, *Parents*, and *Parenting*, among others. She resides in Bend, Oregon.